CAMBRIDGE LIBRARY COLLECTION

Books of enduring scholarly value

Cambridge

The city of Cambridge received its royal charter in 1201, having already been home to Britons, Romans and Anglo-Saxons for many centuries. Cambridge University was founded soon afterwards and celebrates its octocentenary in 2009. This series explores the history and influence of Cambridge as a centre of science, learning, and discovery, its contributions to national and global politics and culture, and its inevitable controversies and scandals.

Fitzwilliam Museum McClean Bequest

Frank McClean (1837–1904) was not only a civil engineer, astronomer and pioneer of objective prism spectrography, but also an accomplished and systematic collector of ancient and medieval art. McClean's collections, which were left to the Fitzwilliam Museum, Cambridge, on his death, were at that time the most notable bequest since the Museum's foundation. They included illuminated manuscripts, early printed books, and the ancient and medieval decorative objects described in this catalogue. The medieval applied arts in particular were of immense value to the Museum's holdings, representing extremely rare items not hitherto represented in it. This catalogue, prepared by O. M. Dalton, assistant keeper of British and medieval antiquities at the British Museum, in 1911-12, lists over 140 items: ivory carvings, enamels, jewellery, gems and a smaller number of Chinese, Japanese and Egyptian objects.

T0381649

Cambridge University Press has long been a pioneer in the reissuing of out-of-print titles from its own backlist, producing digital reprints of books that are still sought after by scholars and students but could not be reprinted economically using traditional technology. The Cambridge Library Collection extends this activity to a wider range of books which are still of importance to researchers and professionals, either for the source material they contain, or as landmarks in the history of their academic discipline.

Drawing from the world-renowned collections in the Cambridge University Library, and guided by the advice of experts in each subject area, Cambridge University Press is using state-of-the-art scanning machines in its own Printing House to capture the content of each book selected for inclusion. The files are processed to give a consistently clear, crisp image, and the books finished to the high quality standard for which the Press is recognised around the world. The latest print-on-demand technology ensures that the books will remain available indefinitely, and that orders for single or multiple copies can quickly be supplied.

The Cambridge Library Collection will bring back to life books of enduring scholarly value across a wide range of disciplines in the humanities and social sciences and in science and technology.

Fitzwilliam Museum
McClean Bequest

Catalogue of the Mediaeval Ivories, Enamels, Jewellery, Gems and Miscellaneous Objects Bequeathed to the Museum by Frank McClean, M.A., F.R.S.

O.M. DALTON

CAMBRIDGE
UNIVERSITY PRESS

CAMBRIDGE UNIVERSITY PRESS

Cambridge New York Melbourne Madrid Cape Town Singapore São Paolo Delhi

Published in the United States of America by Cambridge University Press, New York

www.cambridge.org
Information on this title: www.cambridge.org/9781108004411

© in this compilation Cambridge University Press 2009

This edition first published 1912
This digitally printed version 2009

ISBN 978-1-108-00441-1

FITZWILLIAM MUSEUM

McCLEAN BEQUEST

CAMBRIDGE UNIVERSITY PRESS
London: FETTER LANE, E.C.
C. F. CLAY, Manager

Edinburgh: 100, PRINCES STREET
Berlin: A. ASHER AND CO.
Leipzig: F. A. BROCKHAUS
New York: G. P. PUTNAM'S SONS
Bombay and Calcutta: MACMILLAN AND CO., Ltd.

FITZWILLIAM MUSEUM

M^cCLEAN BEQUEST

CATALOGUE

OF THE

MEDIAEVAL IVORIES, ENAMELS, JEWELLERY,
GEMS AND MISCELLANEOUS OBJECTS
BEQUEATHED TO THE MUSEUM
BY FRANK M^cCLEAN, M.A., F.R.S.

BY

O. M. DALTON, M.A.

Cambridge:
at the University Press
1912

Cambridge:

PRINTED BY JOHN CLAY, M.A.
AT THE UNIVERSITY PRESS

PREFACE

THE present catalogue, though limited in extent, is concerned with objects of a kind presenting peculiar difficulties; I cannot claim to have surmounted all of these or to have avoided all the errors besetting the classification of similar works of art.

In the Introduction I have tried to summarize our present knowledge, and to provide such references to the literature of each subject as will enable the reader to consult original sources of information.

I wish to express my great indebtedness to Dr Montague James and Mr S. C. Cockerell for kind assistance rendered at various times during the preparation of the work, and in an especial degree to Dr C. H. Read of the British Museum, who has examined the collection with me and placed his wide knowledge freely at my disposal. The descriptions of nos. 108—109 and of the Egyptian, Assyrian and Babylonian objects, nos. 119—143, have been supplied by Mr F. W. Green, the Honorary Keeper of the Egyptian Department in the Fitzwilliam Museum.

O. M. D.

BRITISH MUSEUM,
1911.

TABLE OF CONTENTS

		PAGE
LIST OF PLATES .	. . . . . .	viii
INTRODUCTION	. . . .	I
CATALOGUE	. . . .	78
	Jewellery and Engraved Gems . . .	78
	Ivory Carvings	84
	Enamels	100
	Various Objects	117
	Chinese and Japanese Objects . . .	122
	Egyptian Antiquities	124
	Assyrian and Babylonian Antiquities . .	128
INDEX	. . . .	129

LIST OF PLATES

I. Prehistoric and early Teutonic jewellery.

II. Gold brooch from Faversham; 7th century. Frankish buckle; 8th century.

III. Jutish and Frankish jewellery of the 7th and 8th centuries.

IV. Carved ivory panels; 6th century.

V. Carved ivory panel; Carolingian, 9th century.

VI. Carved ivory panel; Carolingian, 9th century, with photograph of the companion panel at Frankfort.

VII. Carved ivory casket with intarsia; 12th century.

VIII. Carved ivory panels; Byzantine, 11th—12th century.

IX. Carved ivory diptych; French, 14th century.

X. Ivory carvings; French, 14th century.

XI. Carved ivory group; Spanish, 16th century.

XII. Roman enamel; 3rd century.

XIII. Enamelled fragments; Limoges, 12th century.

XIV. Enamelled end of a reliquary; Limoges, 13th century.

XV. Enamelled panel from a bookcover; Limoges, 13th century.

XVI. Enamelled plaques of a bookcover; Limoges, 13th century.

XVII. Casket with embossed silver and enamels; Rhenish, 12th century.

XVIII. Enamelled ciborium; Limoges, 14th century.

XIX. Enamelled brass candlestick; English, 17th century.

XX. Enamelled chalice; Italian, late 14th century.

XXI. Painted enamel, The Adoration of the Magi; Limoges, 16th century.

XXII. Painted enamels; Limoges, 16th century.

XXIII. Painted enamels; Limoges, 15th and 16th centuries.

XXIV. Enamelled ciborium; Venetian, 16th century.

XXV. Painting under glass; Italian, 14th century.

XXVI. Bronze censer; 16th century.

XXVII. Jade vases; Chinese, 18th century.

INTRODUCTION

THAT part of Mr McClean's Bequest described in this Catalogue, though not of great extent, is yet an acquisition of exceptional importance to the University. It contains classes of objects hitherto almost unrepresented in the Fitzwilliam Museum, and rapidly growing so rare that the hope of acquiring them through ordinary channels becomes every year more and more remote. They are the things for which collectors most obstinately compete; they belong to a very restricted group, of which the conspicuous members have been preserved for centuries in sacristies, or have passed in recent times into great permanent collections. The church treasuries, the museums, and the cabinets of wealthy amateurs have between them almost exhausted the visible sources of supply. The finer products of mediaeval handicraft, if they appear at all in the sale-rooms, change hands upon terms which would have seemed incredible to the collectors of fifty years ago.

There are many reasons why mediaeval objects should have thus appreciated in value. Their total number is relatively small, and is not likely to be increased by discovery: in this province great surprises are improbable. The places where the more important works of art are preserved are known; even the typical examples of no more than average merit have almost all emerged from obscurity into positions of comparative prominence. It is not with these things as with Egyptian, or classical, or barbaric antiquities, the sum of which may at any moment be notably increased by the discovery of new tombs or cemeteries. They belong to the Christian epoch; and Christianity, by abolishing the custom of burying valuable possessions with the dead, deprived archaeology of a resource consistently available in the case of earlier periods.

A few tombs of princes temporal or spiritual have preserved for us
the insignia which distinguished great personages during life; but
these are the exceptions to an irrevocable sumptuary law applied
not to the living but to the dead. Christian antiquities of small
proportions have therefore suffered more from the vicissitudes of
time than those of preceding ages: their brief existence has been
more exposed to the chances of destruction. Unprotected by con-
cealment in the earth from the demands of greed or necessity, not
always safe even within the walls of the sanctuary, they were
already a residue long before the days of the museum or the
collector. Such antiquities are, as Bacon has said, "*tanquam tabula
naufragii*,—scattered wreckage to be saved and recovered from the
deluge of time."

The perusal of mediaeval inventories makes it only too clear
that not a tithe of the treasures which once existed has survived to
excite the cupidity of our day. In the centuries before banking
works of art were realisable capital, and, if composed of precious
metals, were too often converted into money by the agency of the
melting-pot. Wars and revolutions, or outbreaks of religious
fanaticism, multiplied risks for all things of high intrinsic value;
the indifference of the Renaissance for mediaeval art, and the
carelessness or ignorance of the seventeenth and eighteenth
centuries, united to reduce yet further a long diminished total.
In our own country, where the Reformation made such devastating
inroads among the treasuries of the Church, the destruction was
even more complete than elsewhere; and but for the fortunate
circumstance that England began to collect at a time when
opportunities for acquisition were still comparatively frequent, the
disproportion between our mediaeval collections and those of
France or Germany would be even greater than it is.

For these reasons alone Mr McClean's Bequest is of peculiar
importance. But in addition to these qualities of rarity and
intrinsic worth, it possesses an exceptional educative value. It
is not a collection gathered at random. The late owner wisely
concentrated his attention upon definite classes or groups; and
although the several series would undoubtedly have been increased
had he lived longer, while certain objects might have been with-
drawn, the groups remain sufficiently comprehensive to introduce

the student to the branches of art which they represent. The importance of such collections is not exhausted by the artistic pleasure which they convey; it is also to be sought in their power of exciting a reasonable curiosity, and of acting as an incentive to individual research. Even when they are of comparatively small extent, they may become the basis of a knowledge which will not only increase the pleasure of continental travel, but may serve a more serious purpose by enhancing the interest of historical studies. Things made and possessed by the men of whom we read in history are a visible commentary upon the written text; they lend an added touch of reality to the narrative; and when their genealogy can be traced back through a long series of centuries, they help in their degree to quicken the historical sense. It is remarkable how much the conception of a remote period will gain in colour and relief from an acquaintance at first hand with the products even of its least conspicuous arts. If, for example, we know that the brooch (no. 4) is of a type worn in Kent when Augustine began his mission, that enamels of the kind represented by nos. 47—59 were common features of our church-furniture from the reigns of John and of Henry III down to the Reformation, that ivories like nos. 34—35 were carved in the great monasteries of the Rhine in the time of Charlemagne and his immediate successors, that the chalice (no. 61) is a typical product of the goldsmiths' guild of mediaeval Siena, we do not merely feel that a certain lustre of great association is reflected upon these objects: there is something more than this. The times in which they first saw the light have been brought a step nearer to us; they have received a new and more intimate significance. To say so much is to repeat a commonplace; but the repetition may be justified on the ground that students who take full advantage of concrete illustrations to history still constitute a rather small minority.

If the enhancement thus lent to historical studies is to have more than a temporary influence, the knowledge of ancient handicrafts must be as complete as we can make it. We should not confine ourselves to the story of the industrial arts, their origin, progress and decay; we should also learn something of the technical processes by which their masterpieces were produced. A slight acquaintance with the practical side of goldsmiths' work or enamelling increases many fold the appreciation of an ancient jewel or reliquary : those who have tried and failed with the most elaborate of modern appliances will entertain a greater respect than the mere student of the library for the Anglo-Saxon jewellers or the early enamellers of Limoges, because they will have learned to understand the difficulties which the ancient craftsmen had to overcome.   There are few who would not profit by a short experience gained in a school of arts and crafts, and by the practical familiarity with technical methods which such institutions have it in their power to bestow.   Unfortunately, the haste and pressure of modern life leave scant time for this salutary alternation of labour ; the interminable tasks imposed upon the brain tend to exclude the training of the eye and hand.   As things now are, it is almost a counsel of perfection to serve even a light apprentice-ship in the industrial arts and at the same time thoroughly to master their history and affinities.   Yet those responsible for education would do well to bear in mind the wisdom of Ponocrates who relieved the labours of the schoolroom by carrying his pupil abroad to visit the various workshops of mediaeval Paris.

In a short introduction like the present it is impossible to attempt an adequate treatment, from the technical side, of the arts here represented ; it must suffice to follow their growth through the centuries, and to bring before the reader's notice the range and continuity of their development.   But it is hoped that these preliminary pages may prove of some service alike to the beginner and to the student already in some degree familiar with the subjects of which they treat.   The information which they contain is not original.   But as it is in great part only to be found, at the cost of much time and patience, in the pages of widely-scattered publications, it may help to prevent unprofitable delays ; while the numerous references to authorities should be useful to those who desire to consult the primary sources.   In what follows, the attempt has been made to present the reader with the essential facts concerning the more considerable groups in the Bequest,—the barbaric jewellery, the ivory carvings, the enamels, and the paintings under glass.

Barbaric Jewellery

THE barbaric jewellery includes examples ranging from the Bronze Age to the later Frankish period (nos. 1—11). But the remarkable Faversham brooch (no. 4) represents a well-defined class with an ascertained history so instructive that we may profitably follow its genealogy back as far as the evidence will permit.

This ornament ranks among the finest existing specimens of that cloisonné jewellery which, as far as our country is concerned, is characteristic of the county of Kent[1]. To the observer ignorant of the rarity of invention in the arts of design, it would appear that an object of this kind might result from a happy idea suggesting itself spontaneously to a goldsmith of exceptional ability; that it might well be an isolated masterpiece of technical skill independent of models and without a pedigree. It would be easy, he might think, to arrange a few pieces of garnet or coloured glass in simple patterns upon a gold surface; there would be no need for any dependence upon others in the conception of such elementary motives; the method of fixing the stones is an obvious method to which anyone would have recourse. But the life-story of ornamental motives, like that of practical inventions, should inspire distrust of this easy explanation. Artistic methods and designs are only modified step by step, like the firearms and the locks of which General Pitt-Rivers traced the gradual evolution. Originality is seldom found, and what appears a novelty is often no more than the reinvestment of an old inheritance. The decorative process here so admirably illustrated is an excellent example of this slow transmission from century to century and people to people. So far from being original, it has perhaps descended through as great a tract of time, and travelled over as wide a geographical area,

---

[1] *The Victoria County History, Kent*, Vol. I, p. 346. See also the same history, *Berkshire*, Vol. I, p. 241. Coins of the period from Justinian to Heraclius have been found in association with this kind of brooch, and the elaborate examples probably date from about the year A.D. 600. Fine collections of Kentish antiquities, including cell-work brooches, are to be seen in the British Museum, the Canterbury Museum, and the Free Public Museums, Liverpool.

as any other process with which we are familiar. Its story is
a classic instance of that universal tendency to repetition and
imitation which makes the appearance of fresh motives in decorative art so rare. Convinced by experience that men seldom try to
create when they can conveniently borrow, the archaeologist, confronted with a process or a pattern which is not childishly simple,
immediately searches for its antecedents, and following it back
along the course of its development, endeavours to discover the
distant sources to which it owes its distinctive character. He may
not always succeed in picking up the trail, but in almost every
case a trail exists; in the present instance it will carry the enquirer
into each of the three continents of the ancient world. It is worth
while to pursue so remarkable a course, and realise by an example
of almost classical precision, how difficult invention is, and how
persistently the most insignificant discovery lives on when once
it has been found to satisfy a general and popular taste.

French archaeologists have described as *orfèvrerie cloisonnée* the
method of decorating personal ornaments by the use of coloured
stones or glass pastes, cut into the flat or "table" form, and set in
cells or cloisons so as to form continuous designs[1]. For this we
may conveniently substitute the general English term "inlaid
jewellery," rather than the more exact translation "cell-work
jewellery," because the French words fail to describe an allied
variety which we shall find existing side by side with cell-work
from the earliest times. Although in both cases the object of the
goldsmith was to produce a brilliant effect by bands or masses of
colour contrasting vividly with the gold of the setting, in the
second case he did not fix his stones in applied cloisons or cells,
but in apertures cut in the continuous gold plate. The distinction
is somewhat analogous to that between constructed tracery in
Gothic architecture and the earlier form for which the term "plate
tracery" has been suggested, the type in which the apertures are
cut through a solid panel of stone. This second kind of jewellery
may therefore be described as plate-inlay, and it will be understood as included with the allied cell-work under the generic term
inlaid jewellery. It is perhaps not too venturesome to suppose

---

[1] Ch. de Linas, *Les origines de l'orfèvrerie cloisonnée*, 1877.

that, as in the case of the Gothic windows, the more delicate variety was developed from the simpler, and that the two are essentially the same thing, or rather, different expressions of a single artistic effort. Such a development is perhaps confirmed by the absence of this more primitive method in the Kentish jewellery, which, as we shall now proceed to show, represents the latest stage of a method originating in very distant countries at a very remote period of time.

There can be no doubt that the art of inlaying jewellery in this fashion spread across Europe from east to west through the agency of the Goths and of the Franks, the former tribe playing far the more important part in its dissemination. It is equally certain that the early Teutonic inhabitants of Kent imported it from the opposite shores of the Channel; it may be well however to cite a few prominent instances in order to mark the principal stages of the journey. Among the classical examples from French soil are the sword of Childeric in the Cabinet des Médailles at Paris, discovered at Tournai in 1653[1], the treasure of Pouan[2] in the Museum at Troyes, historically associated with the great battle of Châlons (Maurica) in A.D. 451 when the power of Attila was broken; the chalice and paten of Gourdon in the Côte d'Or, discovered in 1845, and now preserved with the sword of Childeric[3]. These objects are closely related in technique to the celebrated votive crowns of the Visigothic Kings found at Guarrazar in Spain, some now at Madrid, others in the Musée de Cluny at Paris[4]. The crowns

---

[1] J. Chiflet, *Anastasis Childerici Francorum regis* &c., Antwerp, 1655; J. Labarte, *Histoire des arts industriels*, 2nd ed., Vol. I, pl. xxvi; F. Bock, *Kleinodien des heiligen Römischen Reichs*, pl. xlvi; H. Havard, *Histoire de l'orfèvrerie* &c., p. 60.

[2] Peigné Delacourt, *Recherches sur le lieu de la bataille d'Attila* &c., 1860; Gaussen, *Portefeuille archéologique de la Champagne*, pl. i; de Linas, *Origines* &c., III, pl. i; Venturi, *Storia dell' arte italiana*, II, fig. 23, p. 25; Rohault de Fleury, *La Messe*, Vol. IV, pl. 284.

[3] Labarte, *Histoire* &c., 1st ed., Album, pl. xxx; de Linas, *Origines*, III, pl. i; Havard, *Histoire* &c., p. 58. For Frankish brooches in this style, see Havard, pl. v; Fairholt and Wright, *Miscellanea Graphica* (Londesborough Coll.), pl. xxix; W. Fröhner, *Collections du Château de Goluchow*, pls. xiii and xiv.

[4] Bock, *Kleinodien* &c., pl. xxxvii; F. de Lasteyrie, *Le trésor de Guarrazar*, Paris, 1860; J. Amador de los Rios, *El arte latino-barbaro en España, y las coronas Vizigodas de Guarrazar*, Madrid, 1861; E. Molinier, *Histoire des arts appliqués à l'industrie*, tom. IV, *Orfèvrerie*, p. 12; R. de Fleury, *La Messe*, V, pl. 389.

illustrate both methods of incrustation, the broad central bands being
decorated by plate-inlaying, while the suspended letters composing
the royal names Svinthila and Reccesvinth are ornamented with
stones set in applied cells after the more usual fashion. The
Spanish examples in their turn lead us back by an unmistakeable
path to the other inlaid jewels which the same Gothic nation left
behind it in the soil of Italy and Central Europe. We need only
mention here the fragments of inlaid gold armour found at Ravenna,
and associated with the name of the great Theodoric[1], and the
inlaid gold book-cover at Monza, perhaps a gift of Gregory the
Great to the young Adaloald, and ultimately presented by Queen
Theodelinda to the Cathedral treasury, where it still exists[2]. This
admirable example of the goldsmith's art, though made in the
early Lombard period, is almost certainly, like the jewels of the
cemetery of Castel Trosino[3], the work of Ostrogothic goldsmiths,
who had attained a degree of technical skill never equalled by
their Lombard successors. Still retracing the steps of the barbaric
tribes across Europe, we find in Germany such admirable examples
as the jewels discovered at Wittislingen, now at Munich[4]; and in
Hungary very numerous inlaid ornaments of Gothic origin[5]. From
Hungary we follow the Goths back to their first southern seats to
the north of the Black Sea. The famous treasure of Petrossa[6] in
Roumania, ornamented, like the Guarrazar crowns, with both cell-
and plate-inlay, is held to have belonged to the Gothic King
Athanaric, who fled from the Huns in the third quarter of the
fourth century, and ended his days in Constantinople. This connection with the tribe of Athanaric leads us directly to the Gothic
settlements in the south of Russia, where other examples of inlaid

---

[1] Now in the Museo Civico at Ravenna. A. Venturi, *Storia dell' arte italiana*, II,
p. 27; E. Molinier, *Orfèvrerie*, p. 13.

[2] Bock, *Kleinodien* &c., pl. xxxv; Venturi, *Storia* &c., II, p. 97; Molinier,
Orfèvrerie, p. 9; Labarte, *Histoire* &c., 2nd ed., I, pl. xxviii.

[3] Venturi, *Storia* &c., Vol. II, p. 46.

[4] *Gazette archéologique*, 1889, pls. v and vi. The jewels are in the Bavarian National
Museum.

[5] J. Hampel, *Alterthümer des frühen Mittelalters in Ungarn*, Brunswick, 1905: see
index s. vv. *Granat*, *Glaspasten*; A. Riegl, *Spätrömische Kunstindustrie in Oesterreich-
Ungarn*, pp. 72 ff.

[6] A. Odobesco, *Le trésor de Pétrossa*; *Archaeologia*, LVIII, p. 267, where other
references are given.

work have been found[1]. We thus reach the third century of our era, and the extreme limits of the European continent. It is safe to conclude from so continuous a chain of evidence that the Goths, coming southward from Scandinavia, where inlaid jewellery was unknown, first learned this new method of ornament in the parts of Russia about the Black Sea, and that they took it westward with them across Europe, teaching it as they went to other Teutonic peoples. They may even have taught it to the rare Roman or Provincial Roman goldsmiths who employed it; for where we find the process employed in Roman jewellery, it is usually upon the borders of the Empire where barbaric influence may be assumed. We now have to ask the further question, from what quarter did the Goths derive the knowledge of this migratory art?

The answer is partly supplied by the Petrossa treasure itself, partly by a most interesting gold buckle-plate from a girdle discovered in 1870 at Wolfsheim near Mainz[2]. This object, which is rectangular with a projection from one end, and thickly set with table-garnets by the method of plate-inlaying, bears upon the back, punched in early Pehlevi characters, the name *Artashshater* (Ardeshir). In form and general appearance it differs from any Teutonic jewel: it is clearly of an earlier date, and from another country: even if it had borne no inscription, it could not have been easily attributed to any part of Central or Northern Europe. The sumptuous nature of the work suggests that the owner must have been some person of high consequence; the proposal of von Cohausen to identify the Ardeshir here mentioned with the first Sassanian King of that name (d. A.D. 238) is not so rash as it might appear, for we shall see that the work is closely analogous to that of a gold reliquary of even earlier date found beyond the eastern frontiers of Persia, in a district removed from European influence. We may either suppose that the jewel reached Central Europe by the ordinary routes of commerce, or accept the conjecture that it formed part of the Persian spoil brought home

---

[1] A. Macpherson, *Antiquities of Kertch*; Kondakoff, Tolstoy, and Reinach, *Antiquités de la Russie méridionale*; *Jahrbuch des kaiserlich deutschen Arch. Instituts*, 1905, p. 57.

[2] Von Cohausen in *Annalen des Vereins für Nassauische Alterthumskunde und Geschichtsforschung*, Wiesbaden, 1873; de Linas, *Origines*, I, pl. i; Molinier, *Orfèvrerie*, p. 15; *Archaeologia*, LVIII, p. 30.

by the Emperor Alexander Severus, who was assassinated near
Mainz in A.D. 235. It will be remembered in this connection that
the Petrossa treasure contains more than one object ornamented
in a similar manner with plate-inlay, while the shapes of certain
vessels which form part of it are oriental; and whether these
objects are of Persian importation, or produced in imitation
of Persian models, it may fairly be assumed that the influence to
which they owe their peculiar character came from Iran either
round the Caspian, or directly across the Black Sea. Communi-
cation between Persia and the south of Russia was established at
a far earlier period than that with which we are here concerned;
and there is no reason to suppose that it was ever seriously interrupted. The products of Sassanian art were widely exported in
all directions. Some of them have been in Japan ever since the
eighth century, and must have reached China by the sixth[1];
their appearance in Germany as early as the third century need
therefore excite no surprise. We thus reach an important point in
the genealogy of the Kentish brooches: they are found to be of
non-European descent. The question now arises in what continent
did their family originate, and how much further is it possible to
carry back their line?

Allusion has been made to a gold reliquary, found beyond the
eastern frontiers of Persia, and similar in character to the Wolfsheim buckle-plate. This most interesting object, now in the
British Museum, was discovered by Mr William Simpson in the
Buddhist stûpa or tope of Ahin Posh, near Jellalabad, in 1879[2].
It is in the form of an octagonal prism, and was inlaid on the
plate system with garnet and pale green serpentine, which stones
alternate in rows along the sides, and form a kind of rosette at

---

[1] In the *Shosoin*, or imperial treasure-house at the temple of Horiuji-Todaïji,
Nara, to which they were bequeathed by the Emperor Shomu I in A.D. 746. In 794 the
treasure was finally closed and has been religiously guarded until the present day. A
very early Chinese figured silk, translating into the Chinese style the familiar Sassanian
motive of the mounted horsemen in medallions, is reproduced in Dr Julius Lessing's large
album of textiles, *Die Gewebesammlung* &c. For the Horiuji treasure see *Toyei Shuko,
an illustrated catalogue of the ancient imperial treasury called Shosoin*, Tokyo, 1909;
Longpérier, *Œuvres*, I, p. 301; L. Gonse, *L'art Japonais*, II, p. 36; A. Odobesco,
Le trésor de Pétrossa, II, p. 19; *Revue archéologique*, 1901, p. 242; G. Migeon, *Au
Japon*, p. 229, &c.

[2] *Proc. Asiatic Soc. of Bengal*, 1879, pp. 77—79; *Archaeologia*, LVIII, p. 261 f

each end. It lay in a cist surrounded by ashes and by eighteen gold coins: within it were fragments of a brown substance, which perhaps formed the relic, and two other gold coins. Seventeen of the coins belong to three of the Indo-Scythian kings whose reigns cover the period from about A.D. 30 to A.D. 150: three are Roman, one of Domitian, one of Trajan and one of Hadrian. The presence of these coins, and the shape of the reliquary itself, which recalls the small boxes worn on chains round the neck by the figures of princes in the Gandhâra sculptures, enables us to ascribe the find to about the middle of the second century of our era. It is therefore the earliest example of inlaid jewellery which we have yet considered, and at the same time the most certainly oriental. Are we then to ascribe to inlaid jewellery an Indian origin, or to seek its prototypes yet further east in Central Asia or perhaps even in China?

The available evidence appears to be against any such conclusion. In the earlier centuries of our era the stream of artistic influence was setting strongly out of India, especially the Buddhist district of Gandhâra, through Turkestan into China: the Middle Kingdom was receiving and not giving[1]. Chinese cloisonné enamel has no connection with our subject[2], and the metal work richly inlaid with coloured stones, chiefly turquoises, for which modern Central Asia is famous, is more likely, as we shall see, to descend from Persia than from the Far East. On the other hand Gandhâra at this period was influenced almost exclusively from the west; in figure-sculpture it was inspired by the late Hellenistic schools of Asia Minor; while in the sphere of decorative art the Persian influences which appear in the most ancient Indian work at *Bharhût* and *Sanchi* had never ceased to be operative. The Wolfsheim buckle-plate and the Petrossa treasure exist to show that inlaid jewellery of the same character was being made in Persia at

---

[1] The great art of China, so wonderfully represented by the work of Ku-kai-chih in the British Museum (4th cent. A.D.), was, as Mr Laurence Binyon has shown (*Painting in the Far East*, 1908), of independent growth. China had borrowed ornamental motives from the west as early as the Han dynasty. See F. Hirth, *Über fremde Einflüsse in der Chinesischen Kunst*, Munich, 1896.

[2] It seems to have been introduced from Europe in the 14th century. See S. W. Bushell, *Oriental Ceramic Art*, text edition, New York, 1899, p. 454, and *Chinese Art*, Vol. II, pp. 71 ff. (Victoria and Albert Museum handbook, 1906).

a period not far removed from the date of the Ahin Posh reliquary;
and it is probably a mere chance that the latter is older than any
specimen as yet discovered among Sassanian or Parthian remains.
The chief interest of the reliquary lies in this, that it establishes
the oriental origin of inlaid jewellery on a firm foundation. Other-
wise it lies in a by-way; and to pursue the enquiry further it is
necessary to retrace our steps to Persia and the regions about the
Caspian.

A most remarkable series of gold ornaments excavated from
the kurgans or tumuli of Southern Russia and Western Siberia at
various times, but chiefly in the days of Peter the Great, is now
preserved in the Imperial Museum of the Hermitage at St Petersburg[1]: the greater number probably come from the region about
the upper waters of the Obi. Many of these ornaments are inlaid
with coloured stones set in cloisons simply massed together or
disposed so as to form articulate designs, and the identity of the
technique with that which we have traced across Europe from
Kent to the Black Sea is unmistakeable. Their production
evidently covered a long period, for the circumstances of particular
discoveries, the types, and the style of the workmanship show that
while the latest descend to about the third century of our era, and
are thus of much the same age as the Wolfsheim jewel and the
Buddhist reliquary, the oldest ascend perhaps to the fifth century
B.C. Among the earliest and most sumptuous of these objects is a
gold penannular collar terminating in the heads of lion-gryphons,
the necks of which are richly set with turquoises in fine cloisons.
The style of this collar points once more to Iran, though no longer
to the Empire of the Sassanian princes, but to the Persia of the
older Achaemenian line. The evidence for this need not detain
us long. The cell-work is so closely allied in style to that of the
well-known gold armlets from the Oxus in the British and Victoria
and Albert Museums, that all these objects must belong to the
same art. The discoveries by M. de Morgan of armlets and other
jewels ornamented in the same manner in excavations at Susa,
dating from the fourth century B.C., prove that this art was certainly
practised under the Achaemenian dynasty, and render it probable
that the royal city of Susa was one of its principal centres of

[1] *Archaeologia*, as above, p. 252 ff., and the references there given.

distribution[1]. We have thus taken another important step: the
pedigree of the Kentish brooch is carried back nearly a thousand
years further; and an early home of the art which it represents is
shown to be the country of Xerxes and Darius.

Down to this point the evidence has been continuous: we can
retrace the course of events with practical certainty, following the
progress of this minor art from Persia to Siberia and Southern
Russia, and thence across the whole continent of Europe to our
own shores. It remains to enquire whether Persia first designed
this form of jewellery, or whether she herself did but receive it in
her turn from countries lying beyond her own frontiers.

The general resemblance in method of ornamentation between
the early Teutonic jewellery of Europe and the ancient Egyptian
pectorals, armlets, and other objects inlaid with coloured stones
has often presented itself to the student of European antiquities;
but as a rule the idea of a causal connection is dismissed as a
seductive but unscientific fancy. Yet this would appear to be one
of those rare cases in which probability is really on the side of the
bold hypothesis, though it may be freely admitted that the history
of inlaid jewellery in the first stage of its wanderings cannot be
established by a chain of evidence quite so continuous as that on
which its later migrations depend. The principal gap which
remains to be filled lies between Persia and Mesopotamia, the
country to which Persian civilisation has always been deeply
indebted. We have no existing inlaid jewel of indigenous Assyrian
workmanship. But we have a very curious piece of evidence which
goes far to show that the deficiency is rather due to ill fortune
than to the failure of goldsmiths who supplied the Assyrian market
to produce this kind of ornament. In a chamber in the North-
West palace at Nimrûd, the earliest of the three palaces in the
city, erected by Assur-nasir-pal (B.C. 885—860), Sir Henry Layard
discovered a number of ivory panels perhaps intended to enrich
furniture, in which Asiatic and purely Egyptian subjects are
curiously mingled[2]. The designs are cut out in cells by the

---

[1] J. de Morgan, *Mémoires publiées sous la direction de M. J. de M.*, tom. VIII;
Recherches archéologiques, 3ᵐᵉ série, pp. 76—82, pls. v and vi, Paris (*Ministère de l'In-
struction publique et des Beaux-Arts*), 1905.

[2] *Archaeologia*, as above, p. 246, fig. 5. These ivories are exhibited in the British

champlevé method, and the cavities were all originally filled with lapis lazuli, the parts remaining in relief being gilded throughout[1]. Now the effect of these panels in their perfect condition was almost exactly that of inlaid jewels in gold; and except that the cells are reserved in the base, instead of being applied to it, the method of production is the same. The strange combination of Asiatic and Egyptian subjects is a common feature of the period when the Phoenicians were acting as carriers of artistic motives in the Mediterranean[2]; and whether the makers of these ivories were Phoenicians or not, it is clear that the process of inlaying with massed gems had been adopted in Asia as early as the ninth century B.C. It is equally certain that the Nimrûd ivories were inspired by the Egyptian pectorals and other jewels, of which such splendid examples are to be seen at Cairo[3], and in the great European Museums; the inference therefore is almost irresistible that the imitation was not confined to Nimrûd; and it seems improbable that the ivories from the palace of Assur-nàsir-pal were only sporadic examples. A fashion so completely in accord with the sumptuous tastes of oriental princes would surely have established itself in Mesopotamia as soon as its merits were known;

Museum, Nimrûd gallery, table-case. Among the subjects are an Egyptian woman holding a lotus and standing beneath a winged disc; a Khepera beetle; personages of Egyptian type on thrones; gryphons addorsed, &c.

[1] Sir Cecil Smith has suggested that the carvers of the Nimrûd ivories, as of others of approximately the same date from other sites, may really have been Ionian Greeks and not Phoenicians as has hitherto been conjectured (British Museum, *Excavations at Ephesus*, p. 184).

[2] For examples of similar hybrid art, especially exemplified in the incised bronze bowls, see Perrot and Chipiez, *History of Art in Phoenicia* &c., II, p. 338 f. and p. 402 (London, 1885). Inlaid ivory work analogous to that from Nimrûd penetrated into Central Europe about the same period. For the examples from Praeneste, Veii, and Chiusi see Helbig in *Annali dell' Instituto di Correspondenza archeologica*, XLIX, pp. 398 ff. and LI, p. 5. See also *Archaeologia*, XLI, pp. 187 ff., and Dr Arthur Evans in *Journal of the Anthropological Institute of Great Britain and Ireland*, XXX, 1900, p. 200. The material used for inlaying ivory in the European Hallstadt period was amber. The process was apparently not extended to metal; if it had been, inlaid jewellery would have reached the west far earlier and by a much less circuitous route.

[3] Among the finest examples are those from Dashur now in the Cairo Museum. See J. de Morgan, *Fouilles à Dachour*, Vienna, 1895. See also Marc Rosenberg, *Aegyptische Einlage in Gold und Silber*, Frankfurt, 1905, where, in addition to the Dashur jewels, the pectoral of Queen Ah-hetep and other notable specimens are reproduced. Examples of such Egyptian jewellery are to be seen in the British Museum.

it would have persisted down to the fall of the Empire, and formed part of the artistic heritage to which the victorious Persians succeeded. If such a conclusion be admitted as probable, the long chain is completed, and the descent of the Faversham brooch is carried back to ancient Egypt, over an area of many thousands of miles and a period of at least four thousand years.

Before quitting the subject of inlaid jewellery, we may note that down to and beyond the end of the first millennium the process continued to manifest its old tenacity of life. It was not immediately displaced on the revival of enamelling in Western Europe, and the two methods of ornamentation are sometimes found together upon one object[1]. The same thing occurs in the art of the Eastern Empire[2], which, like that of the Goths, adopted this kind of ornament from Persian sources. It is interesting to find the old method again employed in Eastern Europe in the seventeenth century, though the stones are chiefly facetted. The spurs, and the hilts and sheaths of swords, made in 1610 for Kurfürst Christian II of Saxony by Johann Michael of Prague[3], are resplendent with garnets in consecutive cells; and similar work is to be seen on the hilt and sheath of a sword of Persian type captured by Kurfürst Maximilian of Bavaria at the storming of the fortress of Belgrade in 1688[4]. As the latter example is also ornamented with cloisonné enamels à jour fixed upon a ground of silver gilt in the Transylvanian manner, we may perhaps assume

[1] Casket in the Archiepiscopal Museum at Utrecht, Rupin, *L'œuvre de Limoges*, p. 35; C. de Linas, *Coffret incrusté et émaillé d'Utrecht*, Paris, 1879. Reliquary at St Maurice d'Agaune in the Valais, E. Aubert, *Le trésor de Saint-Maurice d'Agaune*, pl. xi, Paris, 1872; Venturi, *Storia dell' arte italiana*, II, fig. 76. Portable altar of St Andrew, Trèves, O. von Falke, *Deutsche Schmelzarbeiten des Mittelalters*, pls. v and vi. Gospel Cover from Lindau, Nesbitt and Thompson in *Vetusta Monumenta*, 1885, pls. i and ii (published by the Society of Antiquaries of London).

[2] Reliquary attributed to the time of Justin II at Poitiers (Barbier de Montault, *Le trésor de Sainte Croix de Poitiers*; Molinier, *Orfèvrerie*, p. 40); Byzantine book-cover, possibly as early as the 7th century, in the Library of St Mark at Venice (Pasini, *Tesoro di San Marco*; Molinier, *Orfèvrerie*, p. 43); later book-cover of the 10th century in the treasury of the Cathedral of Limburg on the Lahn (E. Aus' M. Weerth, *Das Siegeskreuz des byzantinischen Kaisers Konstantinus VII* &c., pl. i (1866); Molinier, *Orfèvrerie*, pp. 46—48; *Archaeologia*, LVIII, p. 270).

[3] In the Historical Museum (Johanneum) at Dresden.

[4] In the Bavarian National Museum, with a tent and a number of fine oriental weapons captured from the Turks.

that this sheath was also the work of a European goldsmith. In any case it is remarkable that one of the latest examples of the style should be associated with Hither Asia, the region which played so important a part in its earlier history.

Ivory Carvings

THE ivories in the McClean Bequest are few in number, but they represent some of the most interesting phases in the history of an important minor art. Although two specimens of the French Gothic period are excellent of their kind, the most instructive are the earlier panels illustrating stages in the transition from late Hellenistic sculpture to that of mediaeval times. It is therefore to the historical and artistic affinities of these panels that the part of this introduction devoted to ivory carving will be principally confined.

Down to the sixth century of our era, ivory carving had for the most part occupied a subsidiary position in all the numerous countries in which it had been practised. It had naturally reflected the tendencies of contemporary monumental sculpture and sometimes reveals an astonishing delicacy and power in the treatment of the human figure[1]. But ivory reliefs were largely restricted to the ornamentation of weapons, furniture and objects of domestic use. A change came with the sixth century of our era, when the greater figure-sculpture began to disappear, leaving the smaller relief in wood or ivory to uphold as best it might an enfeebled

---

[1] Almost all the great civilisations of antiquity are represented by ivory carvings. Statuettes of the period of the early dynasties have been found in Egypt; caskets, statuettes, and other objects show that the art flourished over the Mycenaean area; the Ionian Greeks of the 7th and 6th centuries B.C. had an exceptional talent for this kind of work, as the discoveries of Mr Hogarth at Ephesus and of the British School at Sparta alone suffice to demonstrate. The remarkable ivory carvings from Nimrûd, some inlaid with coloured stones, seem to show that Phoenician craftsmen became proficient in the art, unless they are to be ascribed, as above suggested, to Ionian Greeks working for the foreign market. For the Ionian ivories see British Museum, *Excavations at Ephesus*, 1908, pp. 155 ff., where the specimens from Cameiros are also discussed. For the ivories of Ionian affinities found in the temenos of Artemis Orthia at Sparta see *Annual of the British School at Athens*, nos. XII and XIII, and *Burlington Magazine*, November, 1908, pp. 70 ff.

classical tradition. This result was partly due to the growing barbarism of the West, and to that preference for pattern and colour effect over the plastic representation of the human form in which it followed the taste of Western Asia. But the decay of sculpture must also in part be attributed to changes which were taking place in the Byzantine Empire, the provinces of which had from the first exerted a strong and continuous influence upon Europe. Even before the triumph of Islam, the Hellenistic art of the Eastern Mediterranean had been partially orientalised: the Arab wars and the subsequent iconoclastic disturbance bade fair to complete its transformation. It is conceivable that but for Christianity the victory would have been more complete, and that west of China all figure-art worthy of the name might for a time have almost entirely disappeared. But the Christian religion demanded a figure-art, and from this the sculptor could not be altogether excluded: hence, while iconoclastic sentiment and a growing incapacity to work in marble destroyed the prospects of greater sculpture, the inconspicuous ivory continued to be tolerated, and to satisfy a popular demand. The immunity which it enjoyed, the portability which was the necessary consequence of its small size, and the religious character of its subjects, opened to it a free passage wherever the Church advanced, and lent it a greater significance in the history of art than had fallen to its lot before

Between the seventh and tenth centuries the only sculpture in stone which Europe appreciated was a form of low relief with decorative designs suggesting those of woven hangings. All travellers in Italy are familiar with the ornament consisting of interlacings, confronted beasts, degenerated scrolls, rosettes, whorls, and other motives, which cover the chancel-slabs, the ambons, and ciboria of the "Italo-Byzantine" period[1]. It is executed in one plane without modelling or gradual transition of light and shade, and produces the effect of figured textiles translated into stone. And in fact there is a probability that in some cases woven fabrics were actually the models from which this sculpture derives its peculiar character: Dr Lowry has given a curious instance of such reproduction in marble: in the fabric which he illustrates, we find

---

[1] See R. Cattaneo, *L' architettura in Italia* &c.; G. T. Rivoira, *Le origini dell' architettura Lombarda*, Vol. 1; Venturi, *Storia dell' arte italiana.*

a design preserved to us in many Coptic textiles, and represented in the coverings of altars on the early mosaics of Ravenna[1]. The "heraldic" animals confronted or addorsed beside the sacred tree, familiar to us upon Italo-Byzantine and later Romanesque sculpture, are no less certainly of textile parentage. They began life in Persia and Mesopotamia upon hangings, robes and carpets, for the most part disposed within a network of interconnected circles, or in diapers of lozenge-shaped compartments; the stuffs which they adorned were used to cover the walls and floors, to screen porticoes and doorways, and to enrich the attire of oriental princes. Issuing from Hither Asia, they were first imitated in mosaics like the beasts of less heraldic type which had preceded them in Roman times; then, with the sixth century, they won a new lease of life in stone. Just as the gryphons of Bactria, in the ancient travellers' tales, were said to prey upon mankind in the flesh, so their carved or tesselated forms now made war upon the human figure in art; while the scrolls of foliage in which they are often involved seemed to enlace the limbs of man and stifle his independent growth. The eye may still take legitimate pleasure in these intricate or fantastic forms covering the carved chancel-slabs, or framing the church doorways with a decoration of admirable richness; but the effect has always some taint of the exotic; it impresses us as the imagination of involved and inconclusive thought. The sculpture which sets the human form on one level with the forms of animals, imprisoning both alike in bands of interlacings or in the convolutions of foliage, is not the sculpture which can permanently satisfy the soul. In Europe that satisfaction could only be attained by a sympathy with the Hellenic spirit, which did not rest content with ornament, but by the representation of the human form aspired to quicken the consciousness of life.

Against this purely decorative oriental sculpture, the ivory carver stood almost alone as the representative of the Hellenic spirit now enlisted in the service of the Christian faith. Almost alone he kept the plastic art from the degrading influences of the loom. It is hard to estimate the extent to which this obstinate resistance may have aided the first tentative figure-sculpture of the barbaric West, the first Teutonic sculpture which attempted to

---

[1] *Atti del 11° Congresso internazionale di archeologia Cristiana*, Rome, 1902.

treat man as a creature with a soul and not a mere symbol in a maze of ornament. Figure-sculpture on a large scale was among the last of the arts to profit by the renaissance begun by Charlemagne. It is significant that Carlovingian sculpture is itself almost entirely a sculpture in ivory, and is largely inspired by work of small dimensions. Here and there the remains of Roman glyptic art seen by the Frankish conquerors in Italy or Southern France incited their artists to imitation; but as a rule the Franks seem to have relied upon less bulky models; for these could be more easily carried off to the great monasteries in the northern part of their dominions where most of their artistic work was done. The more fruitful sources of inspiration were thus almost certainly the diptychs, the book-covers, and the illuminated manuscripts, which had been coming into Western Europe from the sixth century onwards. Some were introduced by way of Italy, and of these a part were doubtless of early Italian origin; but a number must have been brought by the direct sea route from the Christian East to the ports in the south of France. Even before the sixth century, oriental monks and merchants, especially those of Syria, had been streaming into Gaul and Rhenish Germany: their tombstones have been found as far north as Trèves, and the earliest records of the Western Churches contain no names more conspicuous than theirs[1]. It was not in Ravenna alone that the Syrian ecclesiastic won his way to eminence: the influence of his countrymen was so strong in the West that about A.D. 591 a Syrian could impose his own election to the See of Paris. When the invading Arab conquered their native countries, these Syrian and Egyptian monks emigrated in great numbers to the West; the monuments of the seventh and eighth centuries show abundant traces of their artistic influence over their new compatriots, whose art was still in a more barbaric stage. In Rome itself this influence is one of the most striking features of the dark ages. Various frescoes, among which those of Sta Maria Antiqua beneath the Palatine Hill are conspicuous, afford evidence that the monks of the *Ripa Graeca* had not forgotten the arts learned on the Nile and the Orontes; and not the least instructive feature of the treasure recently brought to light in

---

[1] L. Bréhier, *Les colonies d'orientaux en Occident au commencement du Moyen Âge*, in *Byzantinische Zeitschrift*, 1903, pp. 1—39, where other references will be found.

the relic-chest of Leo in the Chapel of the *Sancta Sanctorum* at
the Lateran, is the consistently Eastern character of the ancient
works of art of which it is composed[1]. If we turn to the dominions
of the Franks, the same influences are found in operation. The
pages of the earliest Merovingian illuminated manuscripts are
covered with designs which originated east of the Adriatic; and
when, with the Carolingian line, the artists attempt compositions
of a more ambitious kind, whole subjects were almost literally
reproduced from earlier Syrian manuscripts. Such books as the
Gospels of Godescalc or of St Médard, are full of Eastern inspiration, alike in the figures and the ornamental motives[2]. Still further
to the West, the illuminators and the stone carvers of Ireland and
Northumbria were borrowing from identical sources. The peacocks
or the evangelists writing at their desks in the manuscripts, the
vine-scrolls with birds in their convolutions on such crosses as those
of Bewcastle and Ruthwell and the Acca cross at Hexham, alike
confirm the historical evidence as to the connection of St Patrick
with the Church of Gaul and the acquisitions of works of art in
Rome by Benedict Biscop, Abbot of Wearmouth[3]. The interlacings
which, like the undergrowths of a tropical jungle, destroyed the
ancient designs of pagan Celtic art, were importations from an
Italy already schooled in what M. Courajod called the "oriental
grammar" of design. The diagonal frets and other characteristic
motives are perhaps of more directly Eastern importation: so also
may be certain obscure figure-subjects upon the high crosses, one
of which seems to have persisted in the enamel upon the Alfred
Jewel, preserved in the Ashmolean Museum at Oxford[4].

The works of art which these immigrants brought with them
into their new homes were naturally portable objects, textiles,
manuscripts, and ivory carvings. We have already seen that with
the decline of classical taste the ivory carver tended to become the
chief representative of the glyptic art in its higher phases. When

---

[1] P. Lauer, *Monuments Piot*, 1906: *Le trésor du Sancta Sanctorum*; H. Grisar,
Civiltà Cattolica, 1906; *Edinburgh Review*, 1907, p. 465.

[2] J. Strzygowski, *Byzantinische Denkmäler*, I; *Das Etschmiadzin Evangeliar*.

[3] For sculpture of this period see Messrs Prior and Gardner's article on English
figure-sculpture in the *Architectural Review*, Vol. XII, 1902. The authors suggest the
importance of ivories to great figure-art.

[4] *Proc. Soc. of Antiquaries of London*, 2nd ser., XX, pp. 71 ff.

therefore Charles the Great encouraged a revival of the arts, ivory
carvings were destined to play a most important part in the artistic
history of Europe.   It fell to them to revive the sense of plastic
form, and to arouse the ambition of the monastic craftsmen whose
numbers were now being rapidly multiplied under the patronage of
the court and the Church ; at the same time the manuscripts which
had been imported with them taught a more extensive knowledge
of iconography and composition.   The ivories and the miniatures
were the chief agents which together formed the schools of
Carolingian sculpture, and the Frankish artist took advantage of
both ; but the influence of manuscripts became almost dangerous
as soon as the ivory carvers resorted not to the Syrian illuminated
books themselves, but to the Carolingian copies of their miniatures.
For the illuminators who worked in the monasteries in the time of
Charlemagne were not always successful in reproducing the pictorial
quality of the figures which they copied ; only the best of them
could achieve so difficult a task.   Many from the first yielded to
the temptation to adopt a linear style with precise contours
and somewhat harsh adjacent colours, the characteristic weakness
of an inexperienced or a negligent art.   Some of the miniatures of
the Syrian Gospel of Etchmiadzin (sixth century) already show its
adoption ; and it has been well remarked that the mosaics of the
Roman churches become more and more linear as they descend
the path of degeneration[1]: the hard, circumscribed forms of the
figures in St Praxed are very different for example from those of
St Pudenziana or St Maria Maggiore.   This relapse into a linear
treatment distinguishes a large number of Carolingian ivories.   In
some Carolingian work indeed, where a plastic original has been
carefully studied, the modelling approaches that of the best
Early Christian reliefs ; but in other cases the artist seems to
abandon the hope of rendering the delicate transitions from one
plane to another, and falls back, like many contemporary illuminators, upon the easier linear method.   He is still a sculptor ;
he does not sink to the level of the pattern-carvers in flat relief;

---

[1] This indolent acquiescence in contour must be distinguished from the deliberate
preference of the great Chinese and Japanese artists, whose significant and nervous line,
instinct in every part with the suggestion of life and motion, is the chosen vehicle of
their national genius.

but he contaminates his work by the introduction of a caligraphic principle.

To the caligraphic school of sculpture in ivory one of the most important reliefs in the McClean Bequest (no. 34) belongs. In this school, the folds of the draperies are multiplied to excess; their borders are often undulated to suggest the fluttering caused by violent action; there is a general effort to suggest a movement often unjustified by the situation of the figure represented. The school is influenced by a group of illuminated manuscripts, known, after the princess for which one of the earliest books was painted, as the Ada Group[1]. Dr Adolph Goldschmidt has discussed the various ivories in which these affinities are conspicuous, suggesting that the earlier among them originated in the lifetime of Charlemagne himself[2]. They may thus be assigned to a period which begins not far from the year A.D. 800; and Dr Goldschmidt believes that none are later than the earlier part of the ninth century. He admits the possibility that the tradition of the style may have been continued into the tenth century, but does not think so protracted an existence probable. (See the note under no. 33 in the Catalogue.)

The difference in quality between various members of the group[3], often very great, may indeed be explained by the varying skill of individual craftsmen no less easily than by the lapse of time, for it is not a safe rule in archaeology to assume that poor work necessarily implies a debased period. Dr Goldschmidt may well be right in assigning the group as a whole to the early ninth

---

[1] H. Janitschek, *Die Trierer Ada-Handschrift*; Sauerland and Haseloff, *Der Psalter Erzbischof Egberts zu Trier*, 1901. (The Egbert Psalter is affiliated to the Ada Group.)

[2] *Elfenbeinreliefs aus der Zeit Carls des Grossen*, in *Jahrbuch der königlich preussischen Kunstsammlungen*, 1905. The ivory panels which chiefly help to decide the date are in the Louvre: the manuscript (a psalter), for the cover of which they appear to have been originally made, is in the Imperial Library at Vienna.

[3] Several ivories of the group are in England. The British Museum has the Sneyd pyxis (*Archaeologia*, LVIII, pp. 429 ff.) and a panel with New Testament subjects. The Victoria and Albert Museum has the large Lorsch book-cover (W. Maskell, *Description of the Ivories*, p. 53; H. Graeven, *Byzantinische Zeitschrift*, 1901, p. 1), of which the companion is in the Vatican (R. Kanzler, *Avori...della Biblioteca Vaticana: Museo Cristiano*, pl. iv). The Bodleian Library has the remarkable book-cover (Westwood, *Fictile Ivories*, pl. vi) to be mentioned below.

century, though the classification cannot yet be regarded as finally established. It remains, however, a possible alternative to suppose that the spirit of conservatism may have preserved the style for about a hundred years, and that some of the more careless examples may belong to the end of the period. The McClean panel is among the most interesting examples of the series, from its evident and close association with the antique. The head of Christ might almost be of the third or fourth century[1], and the rendering of the hair, which looks as if it had been drilled, as it was in the stone sculpture of that period, is perhaps unique in ivory carving. The ornamental details also betray antique influence. The laurel wreath enclosing the mandorla is distinctly classical; it is seldom found in Carolingian ivories, and then usually in examples belonging to this group[2]. The drapery, however, is quite un-classical, and clearly betrays the later and northern origin.

We cannot say with certainty in this particular case whether the ivory carver was inspired by a painted or a sculptured model, though the treatment of the hair suggests the second alternative. But there are other ivories in the series as to which a certain answer can be given to the question. The curious book-cover in the Bodleian Library at Oxford[3] simulates in a single piece of ivory one of those large composite diptych-leaves made of five parts, which were first used as presents to emperors from newly appointed Consuls, and afterwards as covers for books of the Gospels. On each of the lateral panels of this book-cover are three small New Testament scenes one above the other. Now a corresponding panel of a composite diptych-leaf of the fourth century, now at Berlin, has the same three scenes in the same order, the figures being arranged in so identical a manner that a direct imitation can hardly be doubted[4]. In other cases it is not

---

[1] It is one of the late Hellenistic types which disputed the field so long with the bearded oriental head, and for certain representations of Our Lord remained popular during the earlier Middle Ages. See J. Strzygowski, *Christus in Hellenistischer und orientalischer Auffassung*, in *Beilage* to the *Allgemeine Zeitung*, Jan. 19th, 1903; E. von Dobschütz, *Christusbilder*.

[2] E.g., the panel in the Kaiser Friedrich Museum at Berlin (Königliche Museen, *Beschreibung der Bildwerke der Christlichen Epochen, Die Elfenbeinbildwerke*, by W. Vöge, no. 39 A (Berlin, 1902).

[3] Westwood, *Fictile Ivories*, pl. vi.

[4] A. Haseloff, *Jahrbuch der königlich preussischen Kunstsammlungen*, XXIV, 1903.

possible to prove the debt of the Carolingian artist with quite the same precision, though the sources of his inspiration are hardly less obvious. This is the case with an ivory pyxis in the British Museum[1], which in its style betrays a Carolingian origin, but in its subjects is of one family with the pyxes made in Syria and Egypt in the fifth and sixth centuries. So again with the large composite diptych in the Victoria and Albert Museum based upon a lost model some three centuries earlier in date[2].

In these cases we find the ivory carvers reproducing a plastic model. But it has already been remarked that although they would naturally prefer to copy a relief, they must often have been influenced by pictorial art[3]. The history of ivory carving shows a sufficiency of examples in which the suggestion has come possibly from mosaics and certainly from illuminated miniatures. Some of the larger ivory panels of the sixth century are so monumental in conception that they seem translations of subjects in mosaic: a central panel from a composite diptych of the sixth century now in the British Museum, has this character[4]. In the curious Byzantine ivory caskets with rosette-borders, the earliest of which are attributed to the ninth century, we find episodes clearly copied from the original of the Joshua rotulus in the Vatican[5]. But it is

[1] *Archaeologia*, LVIII, p. 429.

[2] See note 3, p. 22 above.

[3] It is noteworthy that some of the cleverest ivory carvers of the Christian period seem to have taken great pains to find models of fine quality. It can hardly be doubted that the carver of the fine fourth century diptych commemorating an alliance between the families of the Symmachi and Nicomachi, of which the two leaves are in the Victoria and Albert Museum and in the Musée de Cluny at Paris, was directly inspired by a relief in the style of the Attic sepulchral stelae of seven hundred years earlier. The well-known panel in the British Museum with the Archangel Michael, perhaps produced in Syria at about the same time, has Hellenic affinities, like the figures upon the sarcophagi of the Sidamara type (*Journal of Hellenic Studies*, XXVII, 1907, pp. 99 ff.), which are inspired by statues of the period before Alexander. So that in the early centuries of the Christian era we find a conscious reversion to Greek models both in work presumably executed in Rome, and in contemporary work originating in the East.

[4] *Proceedings of the Society of Biblical Archaeology*, 1904, pp. 209 ff. The companion to this ivory is in the Collection Martin de Roy at Paris, *Catalogue*, Vol. 1, p. 1.

[5] H. Graeven, *Ein Reliquienkästchen aus Pirano*, in *Jahrbuch der kunsthistorischen Sammlungen des allerhöchsten Kaiserhauses*, 1899, pp. 8—9; cf. also *Jahrbuch der k. preussischen Kunstsammlungen*, XVIII, pp. 1 ff. On a casket at Xanten, the Herakles of Lysippus, which stood in the Hippodrome at Constantinople, is copied. On these

precisely the Carolingian ivory carvers who afford the most striking examples of such literal imitation. More than one of their panels which have come down to us illustrate verses of the Psalms; there is so close a resemblance between two ivories and the drawings reproducing the same subjects in the Utrecht Psalter and other psalters of its class that a direct imitation is indubitable. One of these plaques, on the cover of the Psalter of Charles the Bald in the National Library at Paris, illustrates Psalm lvii. 5—7; the other in the Museum at Zürich, Psalm xxvii. 2[1]. In the first we see an Angel seated upon a kind of couch or bed, holding on his knees a soul in the usual mediaeval form of a diminutive human figure, while to right and left are ravening lions (*et eripuit animam meam de medio catulorum leonum: dormivi conturbatus*). Below, an armed group stands in menacing attitudes, while in the foreground one digs a pit into which men are falling headlong. (*Dentes eorum arma et sagittae, et lingua eorum gladius acutus.... Foderunt ante faciem meam foveam et inciderunt in eam.*)

The second ivory, similarly following its manuscript original point for point, shows us in the foreground a camp and a troop of soldiers. Above, on the left, David is seen led into the safety of the temple before which is an altar with a lamb before it. (*Si consistant adversum me castra non timebit cor meum. Quoniam abscondit me in tabernaculo suo.... immolavi in tabernaculo ejus hostiam vociferationis.*) On the right, a man and a woman stand with averted gaze before a building. (*Quoniam pater meus et mater mea dereliquerunt me.*) Except in the larger groups, where the ivory carver reduces the number of the figures, the correspondence between the relief and the drawing is systematic and exact.

The two large panels of the sixth century (nos. 32, 33) represent in the McClean Bequest reliefs of the period which must have provided the Carolingian ivory carver with many models, though they are exceptional for their great size, which suggests that they may have been made to ornament the front of a bishop's throne

caskets see also A. Venturi, *Le gallerie nazionali italiane*, III, 1897, pp. 261 ff.; and *Storia dell' arte italiana*, I, 512. Prof. Venturi assigns an earlier date to the caskets than that which is commonly accepted.

[1] Cahier and Martin, *Mélanges d'archéologie*, I, pl. xlv; E. Molinier, *Ivoires*, pp. 123—125. In the Vulgate the two Psalms are lvi and xxvi respectively.

similar to the well-known chair at Ravenna. It must not be
supposed, however, that the Carlovingian artist was always a
slavish copyist. The splendid panel, no. 34, the most valuable
ivory in the collection, is not, like no. 34, visibly dependent upon
an early prototype. It is a more original work, of great importance
for the history of vestments in the ninth and tenth centuries, though
not evincing in any high degree the classical feeling for form. The
somewhat hard precision of its style adds to its value as an
ecclesiological document ; but from the point of view of development, it has less significance for the student than the Christ in
Majesty. With its fellow at Frankfort[1], it stands in a class apart,
a work of unique quality, but illustrating less perfectly than many
other ivories the general artistic tendencies of its age.

When next we trace the influence of foreign models upon the
ivory carving of Europe, a new source of inspiration has been
opened to the Western artist. There had been a renaissance in
the Eastern Empire under Basil the Macedonian and his line; the
gropings and uncertainties of the iconoclastic period had termi-
nated in the creation of a new and homogeneous style. When,
therefore, under the Saxon Emperors, Western art underwent a
new revival, affecting a part of Europe which was now definitely
German, models of this newer Byzantine style were at the disposal
of the Teutonic artist, and helped to impress a distinctive character
on his work. The relations between the Ottos and the Eastern
Emperors were consistently friendly : the third Otto married the
Princess Theophanu, a union commemorated by an ivory panel
now in the Musée de Cluny at Paris : and towards the end of the
tenth century we find in sculpture, as in other arts, a conspicuous
Byzantine influence. The McClean Bequest contains only two
Byzantine ivories of this period with human figures, the small
panel with the Crucifixion (no. 38) and that with the half-figure
of Our Lord (no. 37). The casket (no. 36) illustrates rather the
oriental and non-Hellenic side of contemporary Byzantine art, the
animals and monsters with which it is ornamented descend through
the art of Sassanian Persia from very ancient prototypes in

---

[1] Passavant, *Archiv fur Frankfurter Geschichte*, I, 1858, pl. i ; Westwood, *Fictile
Ivories*, p. 448.

Mesopotamia. The animals of similar descent upon contemporary Saracenic caskets, of which the more important examples come from Spain[1], may have influenced Romanesque sculptors in France; in any case the family to which they belong, a family represented upon silk textiles as well as upon ivories, was certainly a prolific source of inspiration to early mediaeval sculpture in the West of Europe. And not to sculpture alone; for the mosaic pavements and the illuminated manuscripts of the time are also pervaded by their influence. The McClean casket, which, from its added intarsia-work, was evidently at one time in the North of Italy, is among the rarer examples of the considerable class characterised by borders of rosettes, most of which have panels carved not with animals but with human figures[2]. The class as a whole seems to belong to the period between the ninth and thirteenth centuries, the best examples, such as the Veroli Casket in the Victoria and Albert Museum, being of the earlier date. Their figure-subjects are largely derived from classical mythology; and they are supposed to have originated at the close of the iconoclastic period, when artists were driven to seek their models far from the usual Christian sources. The classical tradition was always latent in the Eastern Empire, and it may well be that these caskets were brought into being by the revulsion in favour of pagan types to which iconoclasm gave rise; but whether, as Dr Graeven argued, they were produced in Constantinople itself, is a question to which a final answer has yet to be given. They were imitated by ivory carvers in North Italy in the twelfth century[3]; and the McClean example is of the class which may have served to inspire the Italian copyist.

Although the influence of ivories upon Romanesque reliefs with human figures is not so immediately obvious, it is attested by

[1] E. Molinier, *Gazette des Beaux-Arts*, 1898, pp. 490 ff.; G. Migeon, *Manuel d'art Musulman*, II, ch. iv, Paris, 1907, and *Exposition des arts Musulmans*, pls. v—viii. Fine examples of these caskets are in the South Kensington Museum, and in the Louvre, but many are still in Spain, in the Cathedrals of Palencia, Pampluna and S. Isidore de Leon, in the Museum of Burgos &c.

[2] See note 5, p. 24 above. The best example in England is that from the Cathedral of Veroli, now in the Victoria and Albert Museum.

[3] Examples of such imitations are in the Museums of Pisa and Ravenna and in the collection of Count Stroganoff at Rome (H. Graeven, *Elfenbeinwerke in photographischer Nachbildung*, Series II, *Aus Sammlungen in Italien*, nos. 52, 53, and 78).

students of that early sculpture of the South of France which so
profoundly modified European art in the twelfth century. The
monographs which Dr Vöge has devoted to this subject are of the
highest interest : he shows how strong is the probability that the
ivory carving took its place by the side of the miniature among
the models in the workshops of Southern France[1]. But fortunately
it is possible to produce individual examples which bring conviction
even to the untrained eye. Dr Goldschmidt has demonstrated the
close affinities between the enthroned Christ over the doorway of
the Church of St Godehard at Hildesheim and a characteristic
Byzantine ivory carving of the eleventh century[2]. The very rapid
improvement of style in local sculpture during the twenty years
from A.D. 1190—A.D. 1210 can only be explained by the successful
imitation of foreign models, which at that time must have been
provided by the minor arts. Affinities of this nature help the
student to realise how potent was the influence of the Eastern
minor arts in the period preceding the rise of the Gothic styles.
For the ivory carving we may perhaps claim that its influence was
most beneficent of all, because it did most to improve the natural
representation of the human figure.

In the Gothic period the art of the ivory carver enjoyed its
widest popularity and attained its highest technical perfection.
But although the best work is admirable alike in craftsmanship
and in feeling for the ideal, the importance of ivories to the history
of art was destined to decline with the growth of a great figure-
sculpture in stone at the close of the twelfth century. When
the sculptors of Chartres, Amiens and Rheims, of Strasburg, of
Westminster, Wells and Lincoln had re-established the prestige of
their art and left for the imitation of their successors work which
the great artists of Greece would not have failed to praise, the
narrower sphere open to the ivory carver no longer attracted the
highest talent. The *ymagiers tailleurs* who worked in ivory
were content to follow the sculptors in stone, and follow them at

[1] *Repertorium für Kunstwissenschaft*, Vol. XXII, 1899, pp. 95 ff. and XXIV, 1901,
pp. 195 ff.
[2] *Jahrbuch der königlich preussischen Kunstsammlungen*, XXI, 1900, pp. 230 ff.

a distance ; they were never pioneers and rarely masters of the highest genius.   Exquisite though their delicate reliefs may be, they often lack the interest attaching to the ruder but more varied work of earlier times, when there was no great sculpture to over-shadow the minor art, and no fixed canon of style to compel a monotony of treatment.   Two specimens in the McClean Bequest, illustrative of this period, are of great excellence, and one is of really admirable quality (no. 39).   Although in the Gothic period ivory carvings were sometimes used in the construction of large altar-pieces, the majority of those which have a religious destination were probably intended as aids to private devotion.   It is not necessary to discuss in the present place the particular uses, religious or secular, for which carved ivories were adopted: the reader who wishes to pursue the subject will find the information accessible elsewhere[1].   Attention may however be drawn to two points of general interest.   In the first place we may notice the geographical distribution of ivory carving.   The great centres of production were continually changing with the growth and decay of nations.   Within the limits of the Christian era we find the centre of gravity frequently displaced.   At first Italy, and what we have called the Syro-Egyptian artistic province, produced almost all the diptychs, pyxes and book-covers of which the Christian world had need, and it is clear that the Eastern area was by far the most prolific.   But the Arab conquests of the seventh century and the establishment of the Carlovingian power modified this position.   In the East, Constantinople itself became the chief home of ivory carving, though monastic artists living far from the capital in Mount Athos or in Greece may have practised the art upon a less extensive scale.   In the West, the great monasteries on the Rhine and Meuse, and in France, took up the tradition;

---

[1] In the general works upon ivory carvings, especially that by M. Émile Molinier, already so often quoted ; the Catalogues by Prof. Westwood (*Textile Ivories*) and Mr W. Maskell (*Description of the Ivory Carvings in the South Kensington Museum*, 1872), the British Museum *Catalogue of Ivory Carvings of the Christian Era*, 1909, Introduction, and Mr A. Maskell's book (*Ivories*, in The Connoisseur's Library), &c. For the Gothic period the reader should especially consult the chapter by M. Raymond Koechlin in M. André Michel's *Histoire de l'art*, Vol. II, pp. 4—59, and his previous articles, to which references are there given.   M. Koechlin is engaged upon a compre-hensive work upon the ivories of the thirteenth to fifteenth centuries.

but with the tenth century, under the Saxon Emperors, Germany developed a national art, and for about two hundred years the different German schools produced ivories in distinctive styles with few pretensions to beauty, but often characterised by a massive strength and vigour. In the twelfth century the art declined in Germany; the supremacy now passed to France, which maintained it throughout what we call the Gothic period, providing models and setting the standard for all the rest of Europe. The influence of France at this time, especially in the late thirteenth and early fourteenth centuries, was the consequence of her pre-eminence in architecture and sculpture; such ivories as were produced in other countries were for the most part inferior imitations of originals made in Paris or the Northern French provinces. But the close of the fourteenth century witnessed a general decadence: Flanders and Northern France for a time produced work in which the realistic treatment contrasted unfavourably with the ideal simplicity of the earlier age; but the great days of the age were already over.

During the long period of German and French supremacy England doubtless imported many foreign ivories; but she had ivory carvers of her own, and the rare examples of their work which have survived are full of interest for the originality which they evince. We have several ivories of the Anglo-Saxon period, including the seal of Godwin[1], the beautiful tau-cross from Alcester in the British Museum[2], and the curious panels representing the Virgin and Child in South Kensington and in the Louvre[3]. A few ivories remarkable for a certain monumental quality, reminiscent of a greater sculpture in stone, remain to show of what the English artist was capable in the Gothic period: the triptych and diptych made for Bishop Grandisson of Exeter[4], and

---

[1] *Proc. Soc. Antiq. London*, 2nd series, VIII, p. 468; *Archaeologia*, LVIII, p. 412; *Victoria County Histories, Berkshire*, Vol. I.

[2] *Archaeologia*, LVIII, pl. xxvii. For the Northumbrian casket of whale's bone, dating from the early 8th century, see A. S. Napier, *The Franks Casket*, Oxford, 1900, and the earlier books and articles there mentioned; also J. Strzygowski, *Das orientalische Italien* in *Monatsheften für Kunstwissenschaft*, Leipzig, 1908.

[3] W. Maskell, *Description of the ivories* &c., plate opposite p. 59.

[4] Lacroix and Seré, *Le Moyen Âge et la Renaissance*; A. Maskell, *Ivories*, pl. xxxi; E. Molinier, *Catalogue des ivoires*, 1896, no. 122, p. 252, and *Ivoires*, p. 199.

the diptych in Mr Salting's collection[1], exhibit an individuality of style which distinguishes them from all the contemporary work of France. Italy during the same period was comparatively indifferent to sculpture in ivory. In the eleventh and twelfth centuries she produced a few panels and caskets imitating Byzantine models; Giovanni Pisano carved the Madonna which is still at Pisa; but the energies of Italian craftsmen were expended in other directions. The Venetians of the declining fourteenth century preferred bone to ivory, and by combining it with marquetry produced work poor as sculpture but of fine decorative effect[2].

In oriental countries, carving in ivory found patrons down to the fourteenth century. The work of the Moors in Spain has already been noticed: ivory panels and boxes of great beauty were made in Egypt under the Mamluk princes, and the former were largely used to inlay carved wooden doors or the pulpits in mosques.

After the Renaissance, ivory carving no longer enjoyed the prestige of earlier times, though the influence of classical models encouraged a certain development along new lines. The earlier period produced a little fine work[3], the seventeenth century much that was technically admirable, the artists being now for the most part South Germans inspired by the monumental sculpture and the paintings of Italian masters[4]. The eighteenth century saw the art descend to the manufacture of snuff-rasps and bonbonnières, a degradation from which it has only recently shown some symptoms of recovery.

The second point to which attention may be drawn is that mediaeval ivories, like Greek sculpture[5], were always coloured either wholly or in part, and that the colour was enhanced by

[1] Westwood, *Fictile Ivories*, p. 258; W. Maskell, *Description* &c., p. xc.

[2] J. von Schlosser, *Jahrbuch der kunsthistorischen Sammlungen des allerhöchsten Kaiserhauses*, xx, 1899, pp. 220 ff.; Molinier, *Ivoires*, pp. 201 ff.

[3] E.g., the panel with the Triumph of Fame in the Louvre (*Gazette archéologique*, VIII, 1883, pl. xxxv).

[4] For late ivories see C. Scherer, *Elfenbeinplastik seit der Renaissance*, in L. Sponsel's *Monographien des Kunstgewerbes*, Leipzig.

[5] Probably Greek and other antique ivories were also tinted and gilded, though the traces which remain are infinitesimal. See British Museum *Excavations at Ephesus* (1908), pp. 171, 183, 186, 195.

gilding. To our present taste, the actual condition of most surviving statuettes or reliefs, with their fine mellow tone, and the visible charm of texture in their substance, is far more pleasing than that in which they left the workshops. The few examples in which the colour remains approximately in its original condition appear for the most part to lose by the addition : the gilding and the pigment conceal rather than enhance the beauty of the object; and in saying this we really accuse the mediaeval artist of gilding the lily and refining the rose. Yet where, as in the free sculpture of Greece, the colour is only applied to parts of the surface, and that with restraint, we are sometimes almost converted to the ancient point of view. The groups of the Deposition from the Cross and the Coronation of the Virgin in the Louvre[1] seldom fail to exercise their proper charm, and to raise an occasional doubt as to the permanence and infallibility of modern judgment.

Enamels

As enamels are a very considerable part of the McClean Bequest, and are sufficiently representative to form the basis for a historical study, an attempt will be made in the following pages to provide an introductory account of the various kinds of enamelling as they have been practised at different times and in different countries. The important technical questions involved will be barely touched upon, partly because a whole treatise would be needed to do them justice ; partly because in recent years English workers in enamel have published most useful books upon the theory and practice of their art[2].

[1] E. Molinier, *Catalogue* &c., frontispiece ; *Ivoires*, p. 185 and pl. xv ; *Monuments Piot*, III, 1896, pl. xii.

[2] H. H. Cunynghame, *European enamels* (The Connoisseur's Library) ; Alexander Fisher, *The art of enamelling upon metal: The Studio*, 1906; Lewis F. Day, *Enamelling*, 1907. In French the processes are described by A. Meyer, *L'art de l'émail de Limoges*, Paris, 1895. Among general works in which enamelling is historically treated are : N. Kondakoff, *Geschichte und Denkmäler des Byzantinischen Émails* (also in a French edition) ; E. Rupin, *L'œuvre de Limoges* ; O. von Falke and H. Frauberger, *Deutsche Schmelzarbeiten des Mittelalters* ; E. Molinier, *L'Émaillerie*, Paris, 1891 ; *Histoire des arts appliqués à l'industrie*, Vol. III, *Orfèvrerie* ; Texier, *Dictionnaire*

The origin of enamelling upon metal is one of the obscurest subjects in the history of the industrial arts. The application of a vitreous glaze to earthenware and stone had been practised in Egypt from the period of the 11th dynasty; but though the Egyptians were at the same time producing the inlaid gold ornaments to which we have already referred, there is nothing to show that they substituted coloured enamel for cut stones until after the time of Alexander. The systematic excavation of Egyptian tombs has now been carried on for many years, and it grows more and more unlikely that the existing evidence will be reversed. But the meaning of that evidence is that the Egyptians, though they appreciated contrasts of rich colour in their jewellery, and were familiar with the art of applying glazes to earthenware, were not the inventors of enamelling on metal. They did not adapt a familiar ceramic process to the use of the goldsmith, although at first sight it would seem that so easy a change must have followed in the natural course of development. Until recently, this failure of the Egyptian goldsmiths to take an apparently obvious step, had remained a perplexing enigma; and archaeologists had almost resigned themselves to continued ignorance, when Mr Edward Dillon made a suggestion which seems to afford a solution of the problem[1]. He drew attention to the fact that Egyptian glass is a soda-lime glass, only fusing at a very high temperature; although safely applied as a glaze to the surface of a pottery vessel, it would not serve to enamel metal, because the metal would fuse first. To apply enamel to gold, silver or copper, you require a glass in which there is a high proportion of lead; when lead is present in sufficient quantity the vitreous mass fuses at a lower temperature than the metal base, and all difficulties are at once removed. The absence of Egyptian enamels is thus plausibly explained; and experiments made by Sir A. H. Church

d'Orfèvrerie; J. J. Marquet de Vasselot in A. Michel's Histoire de l'art &c., Vol. II, pp. 938 ff.; A. W. Franks, essay on Vitreous Art in J. B. Waring's Examples of art in glass and enamel &c., and in the Catalogue of the Special Loan Exhibition, South Kensington, 1862; Labarte, Recherches sur la peinture en émail and Histoire des arts industriels &c.; Laborde, Notice des Émaux...du Louvre, 1853; A. Darcel, Notice des Émaux &c., 1891; Burlington Fine Arts Club, Exhibition of European Enamels, 1897, introduction by J. Starkie Gardner.

[1] The Burlington Magazine, September, 1907, p. 373.

on fragments of Egyptian glass selected from sites of widely different dates, tend to confirm Mr Dillon's hypothesis[1]. But if a lead glass is essential to the production of fine enamel, the existence of the Greek and Mycenaean jewels now to be mentioned compels us to ascribe its invention to a period certainly as early as the sixth century before Christ and probably much more remote.

Among the earliest certain examples of enamelling on a metal base are the Greek and Etruscan earrings and other jewels of the sixth to the third century B.C., which have been chiefly found in Greece, Italy, and on the north shore of the Euxine[2]. Here we find, together with a kind of filigree enamel contained by applied gold wire, the more difficult form in which the enamel is applied to small figures in the round. It is hard to imagine that a process requiring so much skill can have been mastered without long practice in the simpler methods in champlevé and cell-work; and in view of the remote date now assigned to the oldest examples, we must assume that enamelling was known in the Mediterranean considerably earlier than the middle of the first millennium before our era. The probability naturally brings to recollection certain

[1] Sir A. H. Church tested a number of fragments of Egyptian glass from Gurob and other sites dating from various periods from the 18th dynasty downwards. In a heavy liquid of density 3·28 all floated, though some more lightly than others, this showing that if lead was present at all it can only have been in very small quantities. The heavier fragments were then tested with ammonium sulphide which would have turned them black if they had contained lead. As they remained unblackened, the inference is that they contained none. One fragment only, which in the mass was of a blue colour but had a yellow border, contained, in this border only, barely identifiable traces of lead and antimony. The results of these analyses are not yet published.

[2] For jewellery from Eretria &c. in the British Museum, see *Catalogue of Jewellery, Greek, Roman and Etruscan*, by F. H. Marshall, nos. 1267—8, 1290, 1644—7, 1653—4, 1947, 1951. For the examples found in S. Russia see Kondakoff, Tolstoy and Reinach, *Antiquités de la Russie méridionale*, pp. 52—53, 60, 61, 63, 65 ff. Most of the Russian examples are of the third century, but a crown from a tumulus at Great Bliznitza is stated to belong to the fourth. In his account of the gold treasure found at Vettersfelde Furtwängler claimed a 5th century date for the objects reproduced in the *Compte Rendu* of the Imperial Russian Archaeological Commission, 1877, pl. iii, fig. 34. Other examples of Greek enamel have been found at Melos. The art as practised by the Greeks seems to have died out before the beginning of the Christian era (A. Riegl, *Spätrömische Kunstindustrie* &c., p. 185). A remarkable enamelled gold brooch in the Goluchow collection is worthy of notice (W. Fröhner, *Collections du Château de Goluchow*, 1897, pl. vii, fig. 37).

jewels of the Mycenaean period ornamented with a vitreous blue substance. The treasure of Aegina[1], now in the British Museum, is not later than 1000 B.C. ; and were the blue glass upon the rings which form part of it a true enamel, the centre of interest would pass to the islands of the Aegean. We might then suppose that a Mycenaean art was inherited by the Greeks, and transmitted by them to the continent of Europe, possibly by way of the Euxine colonies. The most recent examination of the Aegina treasure leads to the conclusion that most of the inlay was fused in position, not cut to shape and applied cold. It would be more satisfactory if Mycenaean ornament of the kind could be analysed, but there is presumptive evidence in favour of a Mycenaean origin.

Apart from the Greek and Etruscan enamels, the most ancient certain examples which have been preserved are found along a line running from the Caucasus to Northern France and Britain. The bronze ornaments discovered in a cemetery at Koban in the Caucasus were dated by R. Virchow as early as the ninth century B.C.[2], but some recent opinion inclines to a lower estimate, and would assign them to a period in any case not earlier than the fourth century. Unless we are to suppose that lead-glass was known in the Caucasus at a far earlier period than in the more civilised regions of the Graeco-Roman world, this appears to be a necessary conclusion ; for we have seen that except possibly for diminutive articles of jewellery, a lead-glass is essential to success-ful enamelling upon metal. But if the high antiquity of the Koban finds is discredited, they approximate in age to the red enamels of the La Tène period, of which we have examples dating from the third century B.C.[3] Whether the Celtic enamellers of Central and Western Europe acquired their knowledge of a readily fusible glass from the confines of Asia ; whether it came to them from the South, perhaps from the Adriatic, after the introduction of *vitrum*

---

[1] Described by Dr Arthur Evans in *Journal of Hellenic Studies*, XIII, pp. 224 ff., and again mentioned in *Journal of the Anthropological Institute of Great Britain and Ireland*, N.S., III, 1900, pp. 199 ff. Unfortunately no loose fragments of this blue glass are available for analysis.

[2] *Das Gräberfeld von Koban*, p. 138.

[3] E.g., from Flavigny in the Department of the Marne (*Revue archéologique*, 1877, pt. ii, p. 44). For the later enamels of Mont Beuvray (Bibracte) see J. G. Bulliot and H. de Fontenay, *L'art de l'émaillerie chez les Éduens*, Paris, 1875.

plumbeum; or whether again it was their own invention, is a problem which still awaits solution[1]. A few facts appear to be quite certain. One is that the red Celtic enamel was first employed as a substitute for the coral with which, down to about B.C. 250, the Celts were in the habit of enriching their bronze ornaments[2]. The increased intercourse with the East following the conquests of Alexander, introduced coral to the notice of orientals; and so large a demand for it arose, that it began to grow scarce in those European districts where it had hitherto been most lavishly employed. The Celts were then obliged to seek a substitute, and it is at this period that the fusible red glass first appears. But it must be noticed that at first the Celtic worker in metal did not use the opaque red glass as an enamel: he treated it just as he had treated the coral which it had displaced, chipping and grinding it into form, and applying it cold without any process of fusion. It was only by degrees that he learned to fuse the mass to the metal base, and even then the fusion was at first partial and imperfect. These facts seem to tell against the theory that the Celts invented enamelling, more especially as the masses of red glass found on Celtic sites turn green when properly fused, and green was not the colour which the craftsman and his customers desired to produce. The red Celtic enamel owes its rich tint to suboxide of copper (CU_2O), and it changes its colour when fused because this oxide absorbs oxygen and passes into $2CuO$. Sir A. H. Church has suggested[3] that these masses would yield a red if the enamellers placed a layer of charcoal or a little rosin on the surface

[1] The often-quoted passage in Philostratus (*Icones*, I, ch. 28) runs as follows: Ταῦτα φασὶ τὰ χρώματα τοὺς ἐν ὠκεανῷ βαρβάρους ἐγχεῖν τῷ χαλκῷ διαπύρῳ, τὰ δὲ συνίστασθαι καὶ λιθοῦσθαι, καὶ σώζειν ἃ ἐγράφη. The author is describing a boar hunt, at which the riders appear with horse-trappings ornamented in bright colours. Although Philostratus does not say that the barbarians living ἐν ὠκεανῷ were the only people known to him who made enamels, he seems to imply that they were exceptionally skilful in this work. Mr Franks long ago pointed out that the phrase describing these people is peculiarly applicable to the inhabitants of our islands, where in fact the most numerous enamelled horse-trappings have been found (in *Examples of ornamental art in glass and enamel*, edited by J. B. Waring, p. 14). Continental archaeologists have replied that the word ocean used by so late a writer need not mean the Atlantic.

[2] The whole question of the use and disuse of coral is discussed by Mr Reginald Smith, *Proc. Soc. Antiquaries of London*, Vol. XXII, pp. 138 ff.

[3] The results of Sir A. H. Church's investigations are unpublished.

before fusion, to prevent the absorption of oxygen. The Celtic craftsman may have done this, but if so it seems probable that he learned the device from some people more expert in the vitreous arts than his own, a people to whom his treatment of the glass mass as coral would have appeared the expedient of barbaric ignorance. The Koban enamels are very possibly older than any Celtic enamels which are well and truly fused; and it may be that the knowledge which inspired Koban was derived from regions further to the south. Asia Minor and Syria have never been searched for such small antiquities in the systematic manner which has yielded such important results on northern sites: when this becomes possible, the clue to more than one mystery may be discovered. Meanwhile we should remember that it was in the Hellenistic area during the period after Alexander, that the alchemists turned their attention to simulating precious stones by means of coloured glass pastes. The glass with which they achieved success was a lead glass, with which alone a sufficient variety of colours can be obtained. The fact suggests a connection between the invention of coloured pastes and the discovery of an enamel suited for the decoration of metal surfaces. Should this supposition prove correct, the second birthplace of enamelling on metal may be one day discovered in Hither Asia, perhaps in the ancient glass-making region of the Phoenician coast. On the other side it may, however, be urged that the wide distribution of early European enamels in the districts north of the Alps would be anomalous on such a theory, which would lead us rather to seek them in Italy, a country in more direct maritime connection with Syria. It is further remarkable that the northern enamels are not of the cloisonné variety on gold, as we should expect if their invention was connected with paste simulating gems, but of the coarser champlevé kind upon bronze or copper bases. In the present condition of our knowledge the question teems with difficulties which it would be profitless to discuss at greater length in the present place. It must suffice to have stated the principal facts as far as they are at present known[1].

For Celtic enamels the reader may also consult Mr Franks' remarks in J. Kemble's *Horae Ferales*, London, 1863, p. 185 and pls. xiv, xv, xix, xx; and the British Museum *Guide to the Iron Age*.

These preliminary remarks upon the earliest history of enamel
are not without their bearing upon the most ancient of the enamels
in the McClean collection. Nos. 44—46 are small bronze vessels or
utensils enamelled by the champlevé process, the colours employed
being red, orange, green and blue[1]. Objects of this kind are comparatively rare, and here it is again to be remarked that they are
chiefly associated not with Italy but with the transalpine provinces:
they thus appear to confirm the belief that the earliest European
enamels did not enter the continent from the south, by the
Mediterranean route. The style of the ornament upon some
examples itself adds evidence in the same direction, for it shows
the influence of a taste which is not purely classical, though the
particular motives, among which "ivy" scrolls and serrated bands
are conspicuous, are not themselves characteristic of Celtic art.
It may be useful to cite the principal discoveries of the provincial
Roman enamels, premising that smaller objects (fibulae &c.)
enamelled by the champlevé process are found in great numbers.

Remarkable enamelled vessels of this type have been found in
our own country; the vase excavated in 1832 at Bartlow[2] is of
the greatest interest, while the plaque in the British Museum[3],
ornamented with a columned niche containing a continuous design,
has been held, from the unfinished condition of its enamel, to afford
evidence of local manufacture. In the same Museum are a cock
with enamelled feathers; two enamelled bowls from Harwood,
Northumberland, and Standon, Herts; and some curious little
stands from Farley Heath in Surrey. The inscribed cup found at
Rudge Coppice near Marlborough in 1725 is at Alnwick Castle[4].

---

[1] These are the colours generally found upon enamelled objects of this class.

[2] John Gage, *Roman sepulchral remains*, pl. v, 1835, and *Archaeologia*, XXVI, pl. 35
and p. 300 ; Labarte, *Histoire des arts industriels*, 1st ed., Album, Vol. II ; *Recherches
sur la peinture en émail*, pl. B, no. 6, and *Handbook of the Middle Ages* (translated by
Mrs Palliser), p. 126 ; A. Deville, *Histoire de l'art de la verrerie*, pl. cviii, Paris, 1873
&c. ; *Archaeological Journal*, XII, 418.

[3] Found in the Thames. C. Roach Smith, *Catalogue of the Museum of London
Antiquities*, 1854, p. 84 ; Rupin, *L'œuvre de Limoges*, p. 28 ; *Journ. Brit. Arch.
Association*, III, 284 ; A. Riegl, *Spatromische Kunstindustrie* &c., p. 191.

[4] Horsley's *Wiltshire*, p. 329; Sir R. C. Hoare, *Ancient Wiltshire*, II, 122; Gough's
Camden, I, pl. v (ed. 1806); *Catalogue of the antiquities &c. exhibited in the Museum of
the Archaeological Institute at Edinburgh in July* 1856, pl. at p. 58, London, 1859;
Archaeological Journal, XIV, 282; E. Hubner, *Inscriptiones Brit. latinae*, p. 233, no. 1291.

Passing to the continent we find the Roman provincial territory included in the modern Belgium exceptionally rich in work of this kind; and the discovery of an enameller's furnace at the villa of Anthea near Dinant supports the theory that the district was a centre of production for enamels in the second and third centuries[1]. A bowl with an ivy-pattern, found at Maltbock[2], is of fine workmanship; and another bowl, discovered in a Roman tomb at La Plante, Namur, in 1905[3], is richly ornamented with scroll designs in and about the pentagonal compartments round its sides. This bowl dates from the second century.

From France come several specimens. A vase from La Guierche, near Limoges, had with it Roman coins of A.D. 256—270[4], and with a somewhat similar vase from Ambleteuse, the enamel of which is lost, were found coins of the Emperor Tacitus (A.D. 276)[5]; a baluster-shaped vase in the Louvre comes from Famars in the Département du Nord[6].

Germany and Austria-Hungary have also notable examples. A patera from Pyrmont in the Arolsen Museum was found with Roman coins, the latest of which date from the time of Caracalla[7]: it has on the handle and outer sides an elegant ivy-design in blue, green and orange, with pentagonal compartments like those of the Namur bowl. At Worms there is a cock like the one in the British Museum[8]. A cup with enamelled chequers from Binger-bruck is now in the Louvre[9], and a baluster vase comes from Gladbach[10]. A large gourd-shaped vessel from Pinguente in Istria, perhaps the finest specimen of all, is in the Museum at

[1] A. Bequet in *Annales de la Société archéologique de Namur*, XXIV, p. 237.

[2] *Mémoires de la Société royale des Antiquaires du Nord*, 1868, p. 151 (coloured plate).

[3] A. Bequet, *Annales*, as above, XXVI, 1906.

[4] E. Rupin, *L'œuvre de Limoges*, p. 21; E. Molinier, *Orfèvrerie*, p. 31, and *L'Émaillerie* &c., p. 24.

[5] Rupin, as above, p. 22.

[6] This specimen is very similar in style to that from Gladbach mentioned below.

[7] *Bonner Jahrbücher*, Heft XXXVII, p. 52, 1865; Lindenschmit, *Alterthümer unserer heidnischen Vorzeit*, III, pl. iv, no. 7.

[8] Riegl, *Spätrömische Kunstindustrie* &c., pl. v, fig. 1, and pp. 194—195; *Journal of the British Archaeological Association*, XLI, p. 97.

[9] Lindenschmit, as above, pl. iv, no. 4.

[10] *Ibid.*, no. 7.

Vienna[1]; here the ornament, in the usual colours, is of a very graceful character, differing from the rather stiff geometrical arrangement upon most of these objects. Other champlevé enamels of the class are in the Museums of Speyer, Oldenburg and Cologne[2]. Italy has not been equally prolific. A cup (?) from Benevento, formerly in the Castellani collection, has analogies with the Bartlow situla[3]. It may be added that the "mosaic enamels," with which Roman brooches are so frequently ornamented in the second and third centuries, were contemporary with the champlevé work: the ornament appears to be composed of variegated pieces of glass arranged side by side and fused together, and they are not enamels in the full sense of the word[4]. Large numbers are to be seen in the Museum at Namur, and it is probable that the district was a principal centre of their manufacture. Roman Britain seems to have rediscovered the art of enamelling in compartments of wire, which, as will be noticed later, has a certain affinity with cell-enamelling. A gold bracelet in the British Museum, found at Rhayader in Radnorshire and assigned to the second century A.D., is decorated in this way[5]. Methods of enamelling practised in the Roman provinces evidently persisted in Ireland after the Saxon invasion of England. Mr Franks drew attention to this fact many years ago in relation to the curious enamelled bronze fragment then at St Columba's College near Dublin and now in the Collection of the Royal Irish Academy[6]. Since that time enamels of the same kind in Norway have been published by Undset[7] and others, while Mr Joseph Doran has recently noted their imitation

---

[1] *Jahrbuch der kunsthistorischen Sammlungen des allerhöchsten Kaiserhauses*, I, p. 41; *Gazette archéologique*, 1884, pls. 18, 19; Riegl, *Spätrömische Kunstindustrie* &c., pl. vi; A. Venturi, *Storia dell' arte italiana*, II, fig. 67, p. 81.

[2] Riegl, as above, p. 189; Kondakoff, *Geschichte und Denkmäler des byzantinischen Émails*, pp. 21 ff.

[3] Rupin, *L'œuvre de Limoges*, p. 26.

[4] Molinier, *Orfèvrerie*, p. 30.

[5] *The Reliquary and Illustrated Archaeologist*, v, 1899, p. 259.

[6] *Examples of ornamental art in Glass and Enamel* &c., edited by J. B. Waring, pl. vi, fig. 4 and p. 15. The enamel of this object recalls that of the Roman millefiore enamelled brooches.

[7] *Mémoires de la Société royale des Antiquaires du Nord*, Copenhagen, 1890, pp. 33 ff. and pls. i and ii.

in the illuminations of early Irish MSS[1], especially the Books of Durrow and Kells. Certain enamelled discs at the base of handles on bronze bowls, bearing flamboyant and spiral Celtic designs, have been conjecturally assigned by Mr J. Romilly Allen to the transitional period between Celtic and Saxon paganism and Celtic and Saxon Christianity, before A.D. 650. It is remarkable that all these bowls have been found in England. Here too the resemblance between the designs on some of the discs and ornaments in the Book of Durrow point to an imitation of enamels on the part of the illuminators[2].

The earliest cloisonné or "cell" enamels at present known are those discovered with objects of Roman date in Nubia[3], and now at Munich and Berlin. Between these and the nearest examples in point of time, there is a considerable interval, for although literary allusions allow us to conjecture that such enamelling was practised in the reign of Constantine, we have no surviving examples certainly of that date; while it is not until the tenth century that this method of ornamenting gold attained perfection. Isolated objects, such as the reliquary at Poitiers supposed to have been presented to St Radegund by Justin II and Sophia[4], the wonderful reliquary-cross recently. brought to light on the opening of the relic chest in the chapel of the *Sancta Sanctorum* at the Lateran[5], the pair of earrings[6] and the remarkable brooch apparently made in Italy[7] about the year A.D. 600 in the British

[1] *Burlington Magazine*, XIII, 1908, no. 63 (June), pp. 138 ff. Mr J. Romilly Allen had already drawn attention to the resemblance between illuminated medallions with trumpet-pattern and a well known class of enamelled discs which were fitted to the sides of bronze bowls to support the handles.

[2] *The Reliquary and Illustrated Archaeologist*, VI, 1900, pp. 242 ff.; *Archaeologia*, LVI.

[3] In the upper part of a pyramid at Merawi or Nepata (Meroe), not far from the 4th cataract. G. Ferlini, *Cenno sugli scavi operati nella Nubia*, Bologna, 1837; A. W. Franks in J. B. Waring's *Examples of ornamental art in Glass and Enamel*, *Vitreous art*, p. 13. The most important part of the treasure, including four very broad armlets, is in the Antiquarium on the ground floor of the new Pinakothek at Munich. They are briefly described in Furtwängler's *Guide to the Antiquarium*, pp. 11 and 12.

[4] X. Barbier de Montault, *Le trésor de Sainte-Croix de Poitiers*, pl. i; Molinier, *L'Orfèvrerie*, p. 40.

[5] P. Lauer in *Monuments Piot*, XV, 1906, pl. vi; *Edinburgh Review*, 1907, plate opposite p. 471; H. Grisar, *Civiltà Cattolica*, 1906.

[6] British Museum *Catalogue of Early Christian and Byzantine Antiquities*, no. 267.

[7] *Proc. Soc. Antiq. Lond.*, 2nd series, XX, p. 64.

Museum, and a remarkable little medallion in the Ashmolean Museum at Oxford discovered by Dr Arthur Evans at Risano in Dalmatia[1], are among the rare early specimens which have come down to us. But though it would seem that throughout the earlier centuries of the Christian era enamel had been largely driven from the field by the popular inlaid jewellery, the appearance of very early indigenous examples in the west of Europe implies either that models of sixth-century date were imported from the East, or that inlaid jewels suggested the independent discovery of cloisonné enamel to artificers among whom the old champlevé process may possibly have survived continuously from Roman times. It has seemed to many that such rude cloisonné enamel as that found upon the eighth-century reliquary from Herford in Westphalia, now in the Berlin Museum[2], or the reliquary of St Maurice d'Agaune[3] of about the year 800, or the ninth-century reliquary in the treasury of Conques[4], or again, the curious casket in the archiepiscopal Museum at Utrecht[5], might well be independent of Byzantine inspiration. The early date of these objects is certainly remarkable, if it is remembered that the great influx of Byzantine enamel into Western Europe followed the renaissance of the art in the Eastern Empire, and that this revival was not general until the tenth century. But as in the case of illuminated manuscripts, textiles, and ivory carvings, we may have here to presuppose lost originals of the earlier Byzantine period which culminated in the sixth century, though it is an anomalous position that the models of this period, if models there were, have almost all disappeared, while several of the Western imitations have survived. The question is almost insoluble on present evidence. All that we can say is that the proved influence of the East in the case of

---

[1] *Archaeologia*, XLVIII, pp. 49 ff.: fig. on p. 50.

[2] O. von Falke and H. Frauberger, *Deutsche Schmelzarbeiten des Mittelalters*, pl. i, Frankfurt, 1904 ; Molinier, *Orfèvrerie*, pp. 24—26, 74—75 ; C. de Linas, *Émaillerie, métallurgie, toreutique: les Expositions rétrospectives* &c., p. 107.

[3] E. Aubert, *Le trésor de Saint-Maurice d'Agaune* 11; A. Venturi, *Storia dell' arte italiana*, II, fig. 76.

E. Rupin, *L'œuvre de Limoges*, pls. ii and iv.

[5] Discussed by C. de Linas in an article originally published in the *Revue de l'Art Chrétien* and reprinted Paris-Arras, 1879.

other minor arts justifies us in assuming its probable existence in the case of cell-enamels also[1].

The great period of Byzantine cell-enamelling begins at Constantinople in the tenth century when gold plaques or medallions were decorated with figures of sacred persons, saints and princes, or with purely ornamental motives, for the enrichment of altars, book-covers, chalices and other objects. The best work was done in the first half of the eleventh century, after which there was a gradual decline, until the sack of Constantinople in 1204 inflicted a fatal blow upon the industry. But in the three centuries during which it flourished, its production was exceedingly large, and examples of the work, unfortunately rare in England[2], are numerous upon the continent. The most conspicuous pieces are those in the Reiche Capelle at Munich, in the treasury of St Mark's, and in the Marcian Library at Venice. But there are numerous other examples in other countries, notably in Germany, Austria and the Russian Empire, most of which are enumerated in Professor Kondakoff's monumental work[3].

Cloisonné enamelling was introduced into mediaeval Russia

---

[1] The earliest cloisonné enamels of Europe, which include those on the iron crown at Monza and the paliotto of Sant' Ambrogio at Milan, are discussed by F. Bock, *Byzantinische Zellenschmelze* &c., Aachen, 1896; Kondakoff, *Geschichte und Denkmäler des byzantinischen Émails*; Labarte, *Histoire des arts industriels* and *Recherches sur la peinture en émail*; Molinier, *Orfèvrerie*, and *Exposition rétrospective*; the works of C. de Linas already cited; Falke and Frauberger, *Deutsche Schmelzarbeiten*; W. A. Neumann, *Der Reliquienschatz des Hauses Braunschweig-Lüneburg*; in which works references to other publications will be found. The lamb upon the large ivory book-cover in the Cathedral of Milan is now considered to be orfèvrerie cloisonnée and not enamel. For the iron crown, *see* B. de Montault, *Rev. de l'art Chrétien*, 1900, pp. 377 ff.

[2] At the Victoria and Albert Museum is the Beresford Hope cross (*Archaeological Journal*, VIII, p. 51; *Manchester Art Treasures Exhibition*, 1857, *Vitreous Art*, pl. vi, fig. 1; F. Bock, p. 350; Kondakoff, as above, p. 176. It is a primitive example, placed by some as early as the 8th century. In the British Museum are two medallions in copper with busts of two saints (see below, p. 47, n. 3), rare examples of the type in which the enamel covers both sides, and two diminutive gold medallions. An interesting gold medallion in the same collection, with a bust of Our Lord, is not of pure Byzantine workmanship and may have been made in Italy.

[3] This book, an *édition de luxe*, is published both in French and German. It is based upon the enamels of the Swenigorodskoi Collection, which also form the text of F. Bock's *Die byzantinischen Zellenschmelze...der Sammlung Swenigorodskoi*, Aix-la-Chapelle, 1896.

with Christianity, and examples of the tenth and eleventh centuries are described by Kondakoff. Though the art was probably destroyed by the Mongol invasions, the old tradition has been restored in modern times and ikons made in our own day afford sumptuous examples of the style. A most remarkable copper basin enamelled by the cloisonné process in the Ferdinandeum at Innsbruck, and bearing an Arabic inscription with the name of an Urtukide prince reigning in the first half of the twelfth century, shows the extension of the Byzantine style to the Saracenic area[1]. To the cloisonné enamels of the Eastern Empire must also be affiliated the examples made in Sicily[2], and in Central Europe, especially on the Rhine[3]. In the latter region they begin to appear in the time of Otto III and Archbishop Egbert of Trèves, and examples of historical importance are still at Trèves itself, at Essen and in other German cities. They were made in considerable quantities until the close of the twelfth century, when the triumph of the champlevé process was assured. Examples of the period now in England are a circular brooch in the British Museum[4], and the magnificent book-cover known as the Sion book-cover, in the Victoria and Albert Museum at South Kensington[5]. Cloisonné enamelling was early adopted by Saracenic craftsmen, who first became acquainted with it through their contact with Byzantine artists. The copper dish at Innsbruck has been mentioned above, but the process was also a favourite with the Moorish goldsmiths in Spain, and the hilts of the swords of Boabdil are

[1] G. Migeon, *Gazette des Beaux-Arts*, 3rd period, XXXV, p. 206, and plate; O. von Falke, *Monatshefte für Kunstwissenschaft*, 1909, pp. 234 ff.; Van Berchem and Strzygowski, *Amida*, pp. 120, 348.

[2] Examples on the imperial regalia at Vienna are reproduced in F. Bock's *Kleinodien des heiligen römischen Reichs*, pls. viii, xxx, xlv, &c.

[3] For the cloisonné crosses at Essen see G. Humann, *Die Kunstwerke der Münsterkirche von Essen*, Düsseldorf, 1904; P. Clemen, *Kunstdenkmäler der Rheinprovinz*, II, p. 42. Other remarkable German cell-enamels of the 10th to 11th centuries are the case for the Holy Nail at Trier, and the cover of the Codex Aureus in the Grand Ducal Museum at Gotha (von Falke and Frauberger, *Deutsche Schmelzarbeiten* &c., pls. ii and iv; Palustre and Barbier de Montault, *Trésor de Trèves*, pl. ii).

[4] *Proc. Soc. Antiq. London*, 2nd ser., XX, plate opposite p. 65, fig. 2.

[5] *La Collection Spitzer*, Vol. I, *L'orfèvrerie*, pl. i; E. Molinier, *L'orfèvrerie*, p. 85; A. Darcel in *Gazette des Beaux Arts*, 1865, 437, 511; F. de Lasteyrie, *Hist. de l'orfèvrerie*, pp. 88—89.

examples of their later style[1]. The method survived sporadically in other parts of Europe long after it had been generally superseded. There are curious examples of horse-trappings associated with Venice which are apparently allied to the Moorish work[2], while the goldsmiths of the Renaissance sometimes resorted to cell-work upon their jewels. The little panels upon the gold shield of Charles IX[3], now in the Galerie d'Apollon in the Louvre, are among the most interesting examples.

The enamel in which the design is enclosed, not by strips of metal set on edge but by twisted wire bent into the requisite forms, is to be regarded as a variety of cloisonné enamel[4]. The principal area in which it occurs is Hungary, where it was practised from the early part of the fifteenth century down to about A.D. 1540. But it seems clear that the process originated in the latter part of the fourteenth century in Italy, perhaps in or near Venice, and that Hungary was only a stage on its passage northward, for fine examples are found in Silesia[5], where the work appears to

[1] G. Migeon, *Manuel de l'art Musulman*, II, figs. 196—198, pp. 240—242. The swords belong to the Marquises of Viane and Campotejar and to the Museum of Cassel. For late survivals of cloisonné enamel in Spanish religious art *see* O. von Falke, in A. Michel, *Histoire de l'art depuis les premiers temps chrétiens*, Vol. III, p. 896. The remarkable enamelled ewer in the treasury of St Maurice d'Agaune, with subjects of a purely Persian character, is by some regarded as of the Sassanian period. Others consider it as of later date but reproducing an earlier model like the small plaques with animals of oriental character in the Pala d' Oro at Venice. It is very probable that the Sassanian Persians produced cloisonné enamels, but the material at present available does not suffice to prove it. The ewer at Saint-Maurice is figured by E. Aubert, *Le trésor de Saint-Maurice d'Agaune*, pls. xix—xxi; M. Dieulafoy, *L'art antique de la Perse*, V, pp. 158—159. See also Kondakoff, *Geschichte und Denkmäler des byzantinischen Émails*, p. 226; and A. Odobesco, *Le trésor de Pétrossa*, II, p. 26.

[2] *Proc. Soc. Antiq. London*, XXI, p. 376.

[3] Barbet de Jouy, *Notice du Musée des Souverains*, no. 69; A. Darcel, *Notice des Émaux &c.*, 1891, pp. 422, 582.

[4] J. Hampel, *Das mittelalterliche Drahtemail*, Budapest, 1888; E. de Radisics, *Gazette des Beaux-Arts*, 3rd period, XXIV, p. 276; Pulszky, Radisics and Molinier, *Chefs d'œuvres d'orfèvrerie à l'exposition de Budapest*, 1884; E. Szalay, *Die historischen Denkmäler Ungarn's in der* 1896er. *Millennium's Landesausstellung*, II, pp. 228 ff.; *Gazette archéologique*, Paris, 1884, p. 351. The earliest Hungarian example is the sword of Frederick Duke of Saxony, made at Ofen in A.D. 1425, and now in the Historical Museum at Dresden. For earlier Italian work see O. von Falke in A. Michel, *Histoire de l'art*, III, p. 894.

[5] Crown on the bust of St Dorothy in the Museum of Silesian Antiquities at Breslau; chalice in the Cathedral of Frauenburg (*Zeitschrift für Christliche Kunst*, VII, 1894, p. 139).

have been made. The designs adopted for this wire enamel are usually floral, and the colours are blue, green, yellow and white. The most conspicuous objects decorated in this manner are chalices, of which a number are to be seen in the Museums of Budapest. The process recalls, though on a larger scale, one which had been employed by the early Greek goldsmiths, and by Romano-British enamellers in the second century (see above, p. 40). Enamelling in openwork (*émail de plique à jour*) has also in some of its developments a relationship to the cloisonné process, and may therefore be mentioned here[1]. A fine beaker in this style is in the Victoria and Albert Museum. Here the enamel is intended to be held to the light and produces its effect in the same manner as a stained glass window. But in Transylvania designs in openwork enamel were laid upon a background of gilt metal as a decoration for trappings and objects of personal adornment. The method came into use in the middle of the sixteenth century and continued for about two hundred and fifty years[2].

In the sixteenth century other enamels were made in France which have resemblance to cell-work, and may therefore be mentioned here. An ornamental motive—in the style of Étienne de Laulne or some other *maître ornemaniste*—was cut in a glass paste; the cavities were then lined with thin gold, and filled with enamel of various colours. After firing and polishing, the edges of the gold linings remain conspicuous, and serve to accentuate the contours of the design, giving the whole the appearance of cell-enamel: a foil, usually of some deep colour such as a rich blue, was applied to the back, to give a satisfactory ground. Enamels of this kind were commonly round or oval, and were sometimes set in the backs of watch cases. A watch thus ornamented is in the British Museum, where there are two other examples of this kind of work[3]. The method has some analogy to one employed in Ireland at a far earlier period. The Ardagh chalice[4] has upon it

---

[1] For the process see L. Day, *Enamelling*. Enamel of this kind has been practised with much success in modern times, especially at Copenhagen.

[2] Numerous examples are in the National Museum at Budapest.

[3] *Guide to the Mediaeval Room*, fig. 15.

[4] *Transactions of the Royal Irish Academy*, XXIV, pt. ii; *Archaeological Journal*, XXVI, p. 290; M. Stokes, *Early Christian Art in Ireland*, fig. 31, p. 83 (Handbook of

discs of enamel in which are intaglio designs filled with enamel of a different colour, though in this case there are no gold linings to the cavities.

Cloisonné enamelling is a process best adapted to the precious metals, more especially to gold: it is therefore very costly, and when enamellers desired to ornament considerable surfaces with colour they had to adopt another method. It is doubtful whether the tradition of the champlevé work of Roman times had persisted into the earlier Middle Ages (see p. 42); even if it had, the sight of a stray surviving example might have suggested to later enamellers a more economical method, though it is perhaps more natural to suppose that they experimented for themselves, and arrived at the results already known to the Romans by an independent process of discovery. In the curious reliquary in the treasury of Conques, made for Pepin of Aquitaine, and dating from the first half of the ninth century, the wings of the eagles upon the roof are in cell-work, while the plaques upon the sides are champlevé in *gold*, a very exceptional base[1]. The portable altar of the eleventh century in the same treasure, with cloisonné enamels in copper, appears to be an experimental work[2]; other very curious early enamels are in existence made with copper cells and on a copper base, the goldsmiths evidently aiming at economy, as had been done in very rare cases by Byzantine enamellers[3]. The British Museum has

the South Kensington Museum, 1886). An electrotype reproduction of the chalice is in the Victoria and Albert Museum. Rohault de Fleury, *La Messe*, Vol. IV, pl. 299.

[1] C. de Linas, *Gazette archéologique*, 1887; Rupin, *L'œuvre de Limoges*, pl. ii; see also Darcel, *Le trésor de l'église de Conques*, 1861; E. Molinier, *L'exposition rétrospective de 1900*, p. 61 f., and *Orfèvrerie* (pl. iii &c.). The reliquary of Pepin has points in common with the eagle-shaped brooch in the Museum of Mainz, and another of a similar kind at Speyer (F. Bock, *Byzantinische Zellenschmelze*, pl. xxix and pp. 384—387; Molinier, *Orfèvrerie*, p. 87). The gospel cover from Lindau has also both cloisonné and champlevé enamels (*Vetusta Monumenta*, 1885, pl. i).

[2] Didron, *Annales archéologiques*, XVI, 1856, p. 77; Darcel, *Trésor de l'église de Conques*, 1861; Molinier, *Exposition rétrospective*, 1900, p. 84; H. Havard, *Hist. de l'orfèvrerie française*, pl. ix; Rohault de Fleury, *La Messe*, V, pl. 344.

[3] Two Byzantine medallions in copper are in the British Museum (*Proc. Soc. Ant. of London*, XXI, p. 195), but the best-known example is the large plaque representing St Theodore, formerly in the Basilewsky Collection and now in the Hermitage, St Petersburg (A. Darcel, *La Collection Basilewsky*, pl. xiv; Labarte, *Hist. des arts industriels*, Album, Vol. II, pl. 105). Among early western cloisonné enamels on copper are a medallion representing Our Lord in the Welfenschatz at Vienna (W. A. Neumann,

two remarkable plaques of the twelfth century with cell-work on copper[1] plaques, the scale being too large to allow the use of gold. But when once the cheaper metal had been tried, it would not require a great effort of the imagination to see that the dividing cells might as well be cut from the solid metal, instead of being soldered to the surface in strips. There are several transitional enamels of the eleventh and twelfth centuries which exemplify such experiments: the work has the general appearance of a cell enamel, with numerous very fine cloisons dividing the colours; but a close inspection reveals the fact that the divisions are not really applied strips, but partitions reserved in the metal base: they only simulate cells, but are really produced by a champlevé process[2]. In yet other early enamels, the greater part of the work will be champlevé, while minor ornamental details, such as rosettes in borders, will still be produced by applied cells: this is a fairly frequent feature in the twelfth-century enamels made on the Rhine and the Meuse. But in the first half of the twelfth century cloisonné enamel was generally abandoned, and the champlevé style which had been steadily growing in popularity took its place throughout Western Europe.

The champlevé enamels made at Limoges and in the valleys of the Rhine and Meuse from the eleventh to the fourteenth centuries form the bulk of the mediaeval enamels to be seen in great Museums; and the McClean Bequest has several good examples of the French style (nos. 47 ff.). The priority of the French and Northern champlevé has always been a matter of dispute. The partisans of the North recall the ancient artistic supremacy of the Rhine and Meuse. They point to the fact that in the time of Archbishop Egbert a cross enriched *adjunctione vitri* was ordered by Rheims from the goldsmiths of Trier[3]. They

---

Der Reliquienschatz des Hauses Braunschweig-Lüneburg, p. 315; F. Bock, *Byzantinische Zellenschmelze*, pl. xxxv, fig. 2 and p. 365); and a plaque in the Dszyalinska Collection (C. de Linas, *Les expositions rétrospectives*, 1881, pp. 118, 189).

[1] In the table-case with early enamels in the Mediaeval Room.

[2] Plaque representing Our Lord in Majesty (*La Collection Spitzer, Orfèvrerie religieuse*, pl. i; Rupin, *L'œuvre de Limoges*, pl. xxi); Casket of Sainte-Foy, Conques (Molinier, *Exposition rétrospective*, 1900, p. 84).

[3] A. Goerz, *Mittelrheinische Regesten*, p. 313, Coblentz, 1876; Migne, *Patr. Lat.*, cxxxvii, 27—29, p. 514.

remember that in the years from 1137—1144 Suger of St Denis had to send for *auri-fabros Lotharingos,* and that the Lorraine of that time included both Verdun and Cologne; they quote the close relations existing between the Abbey of Siegburg in the diocese of Cologne and the Abbey of Grandmont, in the Limousin, relations culminating in the year 1181, when visits were exchanged and mutual services for the dead were instituted[1]. Moreover they observe that in some of the earliest existing work, for instance the plaque with the figure of Geoffry Plantagenet (see below), the colour-scheme is nearer to that of the North than to that which found favour at Limoges. The curious enamel in the British Museum with a representation of Henry of Blois, brother of King Stephen and bishop of Winchester, a work probably executed between A.D. 1139 and 1146[2], in their view suggests by its colouring and its extensive inscriptions Rhenish or Mosan rather than French affinities; while the magnificent inscribed crozier now in the Carrand Collection in the Bargello at Florence, signed by a certain Frater Willelmus[3], and two equally splendid ciboria, one formerly in the Braikenridge Collection[4], the other belonging to Lord Balfour of Burleigh, appear in the same way nearer to the work of the Meuse than to that usually associated with the southern city. Their opponents reply[5] that upon the reliquary of Bellac in the Limousin[6] there are champlevé medallions with animals, gryphons, and a nimbate figure, similar in character to Limoges enamels on the reliquary of Ste Foy at Conques[7], one of

[1] Texier, *Manuel d'épigraphie...du Limousin,* p. 348; A. Darcel, *Gazette des Beaux-Arts,* 2me période, XXII, p. 439.

[2] *Archaeological Journal,* X, p. 10; *Journ. Brit. Arch. Association,* III, p. 102; Labarte, *Handbook of the Middle Ages,* translated by Mrs Palliser, p. 146 (Murray, 1885); British Museum, *Guide to the Mediaeval Room,* fig. 93, p. 111.

[3] *Gazette des Beaux-Arts,* 1887, pl. xviii; *Gazette archéologique,* XIII, 1888, pl. xviii; J. Starkie Gardner in *Some Minor Arts,* London, 1894, p. 72. The crozier was once in the Meyrick Collection. Mr Gardner argues in favour of an English origin for the crozier and ciboria.

[4] Christie's, 1908. Sale catalogue, frontispiece.

[5] E. Molinier, *Gazette des Beaux-Arts,* 2me période, XXXIV, pp. 172 ff., and *L'Orfèvrerie,* p. 178.

[6] L. Palustre et B. de Montault, *Orfèvrerie et émaillerie Limousine,* 1886, pls. i and ii.

[7] *Bulletin Monumental,* 1901, p. 308; Rupin, *L'œuvre de Limoges,* pls. i, iv, v and p. 145. Enamels of the same class in the collection of M. Sigismond Bardac have upon

which bears the date 1137. To this period the relations between
Siegburg and Grandmont cannot apply. So early a date justifies
the attribution to Limoges of the panel in the Museum of Le Mans
with the figure of Geoffry Plantagenet, Count of Maine (d. A.D.
1151)[1], and also that on the ciborium (altar-canopy) of the Cathedral at Bari[2], which is dated of the period between A.D. 1130—1154,
Similar early panels were placed upon French tombs; one
representing Eulger, Bishop of Angers (d. 1149), is reproduced by
M. Rupin[3]. Like the problems raised by the earlier history of
enamelling, the question is one which existing evidence cannot
finally decide.

The principal enamelling centres in the Northern area were
Cologne, with its Benedictine monastery of St Pantaleon, Aachen,
Trier and Hildesheim[4]. Of these Cologne was the most important,
and it was here that the great reliquary-shrines of the late twelfth
century were chiefly made. In the Meuse Valley, Liège and
Verdun were chiefly important. In the former city worked the
famous enameller Godefroid de Claire (fl. A.D. 1150—1169); in the
latter, Nicholas of Verdun (fl. 1181—1205), to whom are due the
enamels of the antependium at Kloster Neuburg near Vienna, and
the remarkable reliquary at Tournai[5]. The enamellers of the
Meuse make more abundant use of the human figure than those
of the Rhine, and the objects which they ornamented are more
various in form and design.

them the name of St Martial, patron saint of Limoges (*Gazette des Beaux-Arts*, 3rd
period, XXIV, pp. 350—352). Others of a similar character from the ancient abbey of
Silos, and now in the Museum of Burgos, are reproduced in *Gaz. des B.-A.* 1906, p. 40,
and E. Roulin, *L'ancien trésor de Silos*, 1901.

[1] Labarte, *Hist. des arts industriels*, III. pp. 662 ff. ; Rupin, as above, pl. xiii ;
H. Havard, *Hist. de l'orfèvrerie française*, pl. xvii; L. Gonse, *Chefs d'œuvres des
Musées de France*, p. 198; *Gaz. des Beaux-Arts*, 1886, p. 310 ; Labarte, *Handbook of
the Middle Ages*, p. 124 ; *Exposition Universelle de 1900: Cat. officiel de l'exp. rétrospective*, p. 31.

[2] E. Bertaux, *Monuments Piot*, VI, 1899, pl. vi ; and *L'art dans l'Italie méridionale*,
p. 454.

[3] *L'œuvre de Limoges*, pl. xiii. See also A. W. Franks in J. B. Waring's *Examples
of ornamental art in Glass* &c., *Vitreous art*, p. 25.

[4] O. von Falke and H. Frauberger, *Deutsche Schmelzarbeiten des Mittelalters*,
pp. 18 ff. ; *Repertorium für Kunstwissenschaft*, 1905, pp. 516 ff.

[5] A. Darcel, *Les arts industriels du Moyen Âge en Allemagne*, p. 30 ; B. du Mortier,
Études sur les principaux monuments de Tournai, 1862, p. 66.

The work of the whole Northern area is characterised by a different colour-scheme from that in favour at Limoges from the last quarter of the twelfth century. Green and yellow are prominent, with blues paler and colder than the rich lapis on which the French workmen so largely relied. The designs for the most part appear upon a plain metal ground, on which are enamelled numerous and characteristic inscriptions; these explain the favourite symbolical subjects, especially Old Testament scenes prophetic of the New Testament, and bear evidence of considerable erudition on the part of the designers. At Limoges inscriptions are rare[1], and the subjects are usually based on the New Testament or on the legends of the Saints: the lapis blue is constantly used as a ground, and diapered with small rosettes, circles and quatrefoils. Enamelling here rapidly became a large and important industry, the products of which were exported into neighbouring countries: it was conducted upon commercial principles, with the result that a high proportion of the work has but little artistic merit[2].

The best period of Limoges champlevé work was at the close of the twelfth and in the early part of the thirteenth century: with the approach of the fourteenth century the commercial character of the output becomes too obvious. In recent years a classification of the various styles has enabled us to arrive at a relative chronology. The enamels fall into three successive classes:

1. Those with enamelled figures upon a metal ground, plain, or enriched with engraved scrolls (*fond vermiculé*) or stars.

2. Those in which the ground is enamelled, while the figures are reserved in the metal or applied.

---

[1] Inscriptions are found on the Châsse of Mozac in Auvergne, the Virgin of Sauvetat, Puy de Dôme, the bust of Nexon, Haute Vienne &c. The last gives the name of the enameller Aymeri Chrétien, who worked at Limoges. See *Bulletin Monumental*, XLIX, 1883, p. 457; *Mélanges d'art et d'archéologie*, 2me année, pl. xxvii; *La Collection Spitzer*, Vol. I, *Orfèvrerie*, p. 86.

[2] Early Limoges enamels are comprehensively treated by M. Rupin in his work *L'œuvre de Limoges*, already so often quoted: references to the early writers will be found. M. Molinier has discussed the early period of Limoges in many of his books, notably in his *Orfèvrerie*, Vol. II of his *Histoire des arts appliqués à l'industrie*. The most recent treatment of the subject is that by M. J. Marquet de Vasselot, in A. Michel's *Histoire de l'art depuis les premiers temps chrétiens*, ii, pp. 939 ff.

3. Examples similar to those of the second class, except that the figures are also enriched with enamel applied in narrow furrows or grooves, somewhat after the fashion of niello (*émaux de niellure*). The first class dates from the last decades of the twelfth century to about A.D. 1230. The earlier examples of the second class are those in which the ground is variegated with rosettes and horizontal bands (cf. no. 50); it is followed by a new group in which the ground is covered by reserved scrolls with enamelled flowers, the first of these two fashions being in full vogue about A.D. 1250, the second falling in the latter half of the century. The types with the doll-like applied figures also belong to this period. The third class begins about the third quarter of the century, and is continued in the century following. To the fourteenth century may also be ascribed a number of enamels in which red is more freely used than in earlier times. The growth of Gothic architecture in Northern France modified the character of ecclesiastical metal-work to the detriment of the enameller's art. The flat surfaces, which in Romanesque times were available for ornament of rich colour, were now restricted by traceries, buttresses and other plastic embellishments, which left the enameller far less scope than before. The South of France did not keep pace with the changes of the North, and Limoges continued to work in a Romanesque style in the fourteenth century; but when at last the new fashions finally triumphed, the city suffered eclipse until the adoption of "painted enamels" revived an ancient industry in a new form.

The Limoges style of enamelling was naturally imitated in the countries which had begun by purchasing the tombs, the reliquaries, book-covers, candlesticks, gemallions and other objects forming the staple products of the district. At first foreigners sent their orders to Limoges, and French masters went abroad to superintend the disposition of their work. Thus the executors of Walter of Merton, Bishop of Rochester, entered into an agreement with Maître Jean de Limoges to make, and set up in England, an enamelled monument at the close of the thirteenth century[2]. But

---

[1] J. J. Marquet de Vasselot, *as above*, p. 941.

[2] Thorpe, *Custumale Roffense*, p. 193; A. Way, *Arch. Journal*, II, p. 171: the tomb itself has disappeared, like many others of which drawings are preserved in the Bodleian

with the lapse of time foreign countries themselves acquired the art, and became in part at least independent of the Limousin masters. In the German area the chief centre of enamelling passed from the Valleys of the Rhine and Meuse to that of the Danube (Vienna). We learn from documents of the existence of English enamellers. The Paris taille-roll of A.D. 1292 mentions " Richardin, esmailleur de Londres[1]," and it may be assumed that there were many others who carried on in their own country the industry which they or their masters had learned in France. Such enamels as the shield on the monument of Sir John d'Abernon (d. 1277) at Stoke d'Abernon are probably English[2], and the champlevé medallions in the British Museum with the arms of the Abbey of St Mary of Wardon, Bedfordshire (fifteenth century), may have the same origin[3]. Nor is there any reason to doubt that the armorial pendants, the "prints" of mazers and the earliest enamelled Garter-plates are of English manufacture[4]. Mr Albert Way discovered a recipe for making enamel in a fourteenth-century MS, in the British Museum (*Archaeological Journal*, II. 172)[5]. But there is no proof that champlevé enamelling was practised in mediaeval England on a scale at all comparable to that which we find on the continent: the frequent entries in inventories afford no proof to the contrary because the provenance of the objects mentioned is usually uncertain. Limoges enamel was naturally imported into Spain and was early imitated there. Some of the work still to be seen, such as that of the plaques upon an ivory casket from the Abbey of Silos, now in the Museum of Burgos, is of the twelfth century, and of an original appearance suggesting a Spanish

Library (A. W. Franks, *Vitreous Art*, in J. B. Waring's *Examples* &c., as above, pp. 25—26). The enamel on the monument of William de Valence is still to be seen in Westminster Abbey (Stothard, *Monumental Effigies*, p. 41; Didron, *Annales archéologiques*, VIII, p. 267; *Gazette des Beaux-Arts*, 2me période, XXII, p. 443). For other enamelled tombs, now destroyed, see Didron, as above, p. 265; Arnaud, *Voyage archéologique dans l'Aube*, 1837 (Monument of Henri I, Count of Champagne, d. 1180).

[1] *Gazette des Beaux-Arts*, 1874, p. 14; H. Géraudin, *Paris sous Philippe le Bel*, 1837.

[2] *Arch. Journal*, I, p. 209; XIX, 285.

[3] *Ibid.*, XI, 29—30. The enamel is however of no great importance.

[4] On Garter-plates see W. H. St John Hope, *On the early Stall-plates of the Knights f the Garter*, 1889.

[5] *Ibid.*, II, p. 172.

imitation of the Limoges style[1]. The enamelled ciboria and processional crosses still preserved in the peninsula are also regarded
as of indigenous workmanship.

Champlevé enamel still enjoyed some popularity in our country
in the seventeenth century. Roundels for the centres of large
pewter dishes, with the Stuart arms or of the Stuart period, exist
in various collections[2], while the first half of the century witnessed
the production of coarser work in the shape of large candlesticks
and fire-dogs[3], in which the metal used as a base is no longer
bronze but brass. These enamels, represented in the McClean
Collection by the candlestick (no. 60), have the peculiarity of not
being finished by grinding and polishing. They were left untouched
after the last firing, so that the surface of the work shows continual
inequalities, a circumstance which in the eyes of many enhances
their decorative effect. The prevailing colours are blue, green,
white and an orange yellow; and it may be noted that work of
just the same kind with a similar colour-scheme appears in Russia
at the same period. As painted enamels were introduced into
the Russian dominions from France (see p. 68), so this rough
champlevé work on brass may have been a western importation[4].
It remained very popular in Russia, and the familiar enamelled
triptychs and other devotional tablets are all examples of the
process. The Hungarian enamels already mentioned are similar
in colour, and in the absence of the final grinding.

---

[1] E. Roulin, *L'ancien trésor de Silos*, 1901, p. 1. For other early Spanish enamels
see C. H. Read, *Report on the Historical Exhibition at Madrid*, 1893, p. 23 (British
Museum); A. van de Put, *Burlington Magazine*, 1906, p. 421. The last-mentioned
author suggests that enamelled armorial pendants found in Spain may be the *Émaux
d'Arragon* discussed by C. Davillier in *Recherches sur l'orfèvrerie en Espagne*, p. 65.
These armorial pendants are found in many countries, and those discovered in England
may well be of English workmanship (British Museum, *Guide to the Mediaeval Room*,
p. 55). Spain furnished some interesting examples of *émaux de niellure* (E. Roulin on
the cross at Villabertran, in *Monuments Piot*, VI, 1899, p. 208).

[2] Several such roundels are in the British Museum, one still in its place in the centre
of a large pewter dish (*Guide to the Mediaeval Room*, fig. 164 on p. 227).

[3] Fire-dogs and candlesticks in the Victoria and Albert Museum; candlesticks in the
British Museum (*Guide to the Mediaeval Room*, p. 123). See also *Gazette des Beaux-
Arts*, 2nd period, XXIV, p. 372.

[4] Mr E. Dillon, however, suggests that this style of enamelling came to us from
Russia (*Burlington Magazine*, 1210, pp. 261 ff.).

The style of enamelling which superseded champlevé in popular favour is known in France as *émail de basse taille*, and in England as translucent enamel on sunk relief[1]. In this variety the design is cut in relief on a silver or gold base in such a way that the whole lies below the level of the original surface. The cavity is then filled with enamel in translucent colours, and as these vary in richness and intensity with the depth of the relief, very beautiful effects are produced. The method of preparing the base resembles that of sculpture in *incavo rilievo* or *relief en creux*, which the Egyptians of all the ancient dynasties practised in fine stone without any idea of further decoration; but the Egyptian work is of course cut deeper below the surface, and is upon a much larger scale. The famous names of Giovanni Pisano and Duccio of Siena are among the earliest connected with enamelling in this fashion; Vasari says that the former made a retable for the high altar of Arezzo, enriched with enamels on silver; while the latter artist signed a chalice for the convent of St Francis of Assisi in A.D. 1290[2]. Specimens of translucent enamel are numerous in Tuscany, and several are in the Bargello at Florence. Special mention may be made of a few examples which are historically interesting. The silver altar of Pistoia[3] is the work of Pietro di Leonardo of Florence, Andrea di Jacopo d' Ognabene, and Leonardo di Ser Giovanni, the first two working at the end of the thirteenth and in the early years of the fourteenth century, the last completing the whole in 1371. The reliquary for the corporal in Orvieto Cathedral was completed, as the inscription upon it records, by Ugolino of Siena and his companions (*socii aurifices*) in 1338[4].

[1] Benvenuto Cellini describes the method in his *Trattato dell' oreficeria*, ch. iii. Gold is a better metal than silver for enamelling on sunk relief, firstly because it dilates less and the enamel is less liable to become brittle and crack, secondly because it admits of the use of the rich reds with which such fine effects may be produced: silver is suitable for blues, greens, violets and certain yellows, but not for reds (L. Falize in *Gaz. des Beaux-Arts*, 3rd period, II, 1889, p. 79).

[2] *Gaz. des Beaux-Arts*, 2nd period, XVIII, 1878, p. 573.

[3] *The Reliquary and Illustrated Archaeologist*, 1906, pp. 19 ff.; *Gazette des Beaux-Arts*, 2nd period, XXVII, 1883, p. 20. The original altar decoration was stolen by Vanni Fucci, whom Dante places in the 7th bolgia of the Inferno. "*Son Vanni Fucci Bestia, e Pistoia mi fu degna tana*" (*Inf.*, XXIV, 125).

[4] d'Agincourt, *Peinture*, pl. cxxiii; *Gazette des Beaux-Arts*, 1877, pp. 582 ff.; *Reliquary*, as above, p. 25; *Archaeological Journal*, XII, pl. iv. It is a large

The same artist was employed upon the reliquary of St Juvenal, also at Orvieto[1]. The names of numerous enamellers of Central Italy, chiefly from Siena, survive upon the chalices, processional crosses, and other works of the later fourteenth century which have been preserved in many churches and museums[2]. The chalice (no. 61) in the McClean Bequest is a typical example in the Sienese style.

Translucent enamel rapidly spread into Spain and France[3]. For the former country it was especially practised at Gerona in Catalonia, at Barcelona, and at Valencia[4]. Perhaps the enamels which were made at Montpellier in this style may be due to Spanish influence, as part of the city was held by Aragonese princes in the thirteenth and fourteenth centuries[5]. But the art soon became popular in Northern France, and its most splendid production is the royal gold cup in the British Museum enamelled with the story of St Valérie, and originally made to the order of the Duc de Berri for presentation to Charles V[6]. Some fine plaques of the fourteenth century, with figures of saints, are attributed to

architectural silver reliquary, the enamelled plaques chiefly representing New Testament scenes, and scenes illustrating the miracle of the Mass of Bolsena. The chief colours are azure blue, green, yellow and violet.

[1] Didron, *Annales archéologiques*, XV, 1855, pp. 365 ff. At Orvieto is another enamelled reliquary of S. Savin by Ugolino and Viva. The cathedral of Orte has a processional cross by Vannuccio, pupil of Viva, and several enamelled chalices (*Gaz. des Beaux-Arts*, 1896, pp. 500 ff.).

[2] G. Milanesi, *Documenti per la storia dell' arte Senese*, Siena, 1854—6.

[3] The earliest dated French pieces are a paten in the Museum at Copenhagen (A.D. 1333), the *lion d'or* of Montpellier in the British Museum, which can only have been made in A.D. 1338—1339, and the enamels on the plinth of the silver statuette of the Virgin (now in the Louvre) given by Jeanne d'Évreux to St Denis in A.D. 1339 (J. Marquet de Vasselot in A. Michel, *Histoire de l'art*, Vol. III, pp. 982—983).

[4] E. Roulin, *Monuments Piot*, VI (enamelled crosses of Gerona and Villabertran). See also Davillier, *Orfèvrerie en Espagne*; Labarte, *Recherches* &c. and *Histoire*; Van de Put, in *Burlington Magazine*, 1906, p. 421. For the "*échiquier de Charlemagne*" at Roncevaux, see J. J. Marquet de Vasselot, *Gazette des Beaux-Arts*, 1897, and *Hist. de l'art*, as above, p. 987.

[5] Texier, *Dictionnaire d'orfèvrerie*, s.v. Montpellier; *Burl. Mag.* as above. For the *échiquier de Charlemagne* at Roncevaux, which may be Spanish or French, see *Gazette des Beaux-Arts*, 1897, pp. 324 ff. For Franco-Flemish translucent enamels see *Gazette des Beaux-Arts*, 1890.

[6] C. H. Read, *Vetusta Monumenta* (Soc. of Antiquaries of London), 1904; *The Royal Gold Cup of the Kings of France and England*; Molinier, *Orfèvrerie*, p. 227.

Cologne[1]. With the fifteenth century translucent enamel tended to abandon figure subjects for the floral designs which we see on the Burgundian knife-handles and other objects of the period[2]. Translucent work, perhaps rather champlevé than *basse taille*, was popular in South Germany, chiefly at Augsburg, towards the middle of the sixteenth century. The gun and powder-flask of the Emperor Rudolf II (1552—1612) are decorated with silver plaques enamelled in brilliant translucent colours with figures of Diana and Actaeon, trophies, birds and flowers[3]. A virginal in the Museum at Budapest, one of the ivory coin-cabinets by Christoph Angermair (d. 1632)[4], and ebony cabinets in the Reiche Capelle at Munich are ornamented in the same manner. The enamels of the coin-cabinet are the work of the Augsburg enameller David Attemstetter. The mounts made for large antique cameos and other jewels of value were often of gold richly decorated with conventional designs in translucent enamel. Some of the most admirable examples are to be seen in the Imperial Historical Museum at Vienna.

There is documentary evidence that translucent enamels were made in England[5], but there is hardly a surviving example of which the English origin is indisputable. The small plaques on the mitre and crozier of William of Wykeham at New College, Oxford, seem to be Italian work[6]; the fine cup in the possession of the Corporation of King's Lynn[7] has been claimed as English, but

---

[1] Schnütgen, in *Zeitschrift für Christliche Kunst*, VII, 1894, pp. 23 ff. Two small plaques are in the British Museum, a larger at South Kensington (H. H. Cunynghame, *European Enamels*, pl. opposite p. 114).

[2] *Archaeologia*, LX (knives of John the Intrepid, Duke of Burgundy); *Proc. Soc. Ant. of London*, 2nd Series, XV, p. 257; and British Museum, *Guide to the Mediaeval Room*, pl. xiii.

[3] In the Imperial Historical Museum at Vienna.

[4] In the Bavarian National Museum at Munich, Room 28.

[5] In 1365 Edward III bought from Thomas Hessey various vessels ornamented with enamel; and in 1370 Walsh and Chichester, goldsmiths of London, made an enamelled cup for him. The mere mention of enamelled objects in the inventories of English kings does not allow us to assume their English origin.

[6] *Archaeologia*, LX. The similar croziers in Cologne Cathedral and the Victoria and Albert Museum are considered to be Italian.

[7] H. Shaw, *Dresses and ornaments* &c., pl. lxvii; Sir A. H. Church and others, *Some Minor Arts*, p. 76; J. Marquet de Vasselot, as above, p. 987. The enamels on the Bruce Horn belonging to the Marquis of Ailesbury, and the belt supporting it, are also claimed as English (*Some Minor Arts*, p. 75).

the attribution is conjectural. The great period of translucent enamelling on sunk relief came to an end with the Renaissance, though there is interesting work of this kind ascribed to the sixteenth century[1]. Modern enamellers have given some attention to the process, but it has hardly attained the popularity of other methods.

The present is the most convenient place to mention "encrusted enamels," or enamels in the round, in which the vitreous ornament is applied to a convex surface. The diminutive enamelled jewels of the Greeks are the earliest known example of the process, which was revived upon a larger scale in France (perhaps at Paris) in the second half of the fourteenth century. The inventories of Charles VI mention enamelled statuettes in the precious metals[2], the character of which is illustrated by a surviving example, a devotional group, now in Bavaria, made for that King, and known as the Rössl of Altötting[3]. It was carried off to his own country by the brother of Isabeau de Bavière, a circumstance which preserved it from the general destruction in which examples remaining in France were involved. Another example of this work is the "calvary" in the treasury of the Cathedral at Gran in Hungary[4]. In this masterpiece the base, which is formed of sphinxes in the style of the early Renaissance, supports the earlier enamelled crucifix. In the late sixteenth and in the seventeenth centuries enamelling on high relief was much practised, especially upon the jewelled pendants made in such numbers chiefly in Southern Germany, and well illustrated in this country by the examples in the Waddesdon Bequest at the British Museum[5].

---

[1] The process was continued in Spain until the middle of the century (pax in the Cathedral of Valencia). Cf. also medallions assigned to the 16th century in the Fortnum Collection in the Ashmolean Museum at Oxford.

[2] "Une image d'or de Nostre Dame esmaillée de blanc, assise en une chayère d'or, laquelle tient son enfant en son giron vestu d'une cotte esmaillée de rouge clère," &c.

[3] Didron, *Annales archéologiques*, XXVI, pp. 119, 209 ff.; Molinier, *Orfèvrerie*, p. 219; H. Havard, *Hist. de l'orfèvrerie française*, fig. on p. 250; O. von Falke, in A. Michel's *Histoire de l'art*, III, pp. 867—869. Some would assign an enamelled reliquary in the Waddesdon Bequest at the British Museum (C. H. Read, *Catalogue*, no. 67) to this period.

[4] Reproduced in Cardinal Simor's work on the Treasure of Gran.

[5] C. H. Read, *Catalogue of the Waddesdon Bequest*, nos. 147, &c. (British Museum, 1902). See also H. Havard, *Hist. de l'orfèvrerie française*, chs. xvi and xvii;

The figures with which German goldsmiths enriched their elaborate ebony cabinets or set groups of figures were also thus enamelled[1]. The most extraordinary example is the great group by J. M. Dinglinger in the Grünes Gewölbe at Dresden, representing the Court of Aurungzebe, in which there are no less than a hundred and thirty-two enamelled figures.

Just as enamelling by the champlevé process was a simplification of cell-work, so painted enamels[2] resulted from a simplification of work in *basse taille*, the processes of transition perhaps varying in different countries. In Italy translucent enamels on silver became shallower until sunk relief was abandoned[3]. The way was thus prepared for " painting," in which the design, instead of being engraved in sunk relief, was first transferred by a tracing to the surface of the metal, and the contours were then covered with enamel, applied not with the brush, but with the spatula. The term " painted enamel" is misleading if it suggests that the enamels of the Penicauds, or Léonard Limousin, are the result of brush-work : almost every effect was really achieved by the spatula or the point.

The new process[4] may elsewhere have been facilitated by observation of other branches of vitreous art. Thus there is a theory that it began in the ateliers of the glass-makers. Here the workmen were familiar with the art of colouring glass with metallic oxides; and when the process of applying enamel-colours to the surface of plain glass began to be understood, the transference of the method to a metal surface might readily suggest itself in any region where enamelling on metal had been practised. Perhaps

W. Fröhner, *Les collections du château de Goluchow*, pl. xxi ; E. Molinier, *Donation de M. le Baron Adolphe Rothschild*, Musée du Louvre, 1902, pl. xxxii; Fairholt and Wright, *Miscellanea Graphica* (Londesborough Collection), pls. i, v, xxxviii.

[1] Examples at Dresden and Munich.

[2] See the books mentioned in note 2, p. 32 ; works by L. Bourdery, articles by C. Popelin, *Gaz. des Beaux-Arts*, 1881, p. 107 ; E. Molinier, *Dictionnaire des émailleurs*, Paris, 1885.

[3] For examples see O. von Falke, as above, pp. 890, 891.

[4] Enamelling in the round, which, as we have seen, was practised in France at the end of the 14th century, has points in common with painted enamelling ; but the scope and application of the latter were so much wider that it may fairly be called a new process.

the idea may first have occurred to the decorators of glass vessels, as enamel-colours appear to have been applied to these rather earlier than to stained windows.   But about the same time the old process of decorating windows was undergoing a change in the same direction.   It had been the earlier mediaeval usage to colour the whole body of the glass with metallic oxides, then to fit together small pieces, each stained with one tint only, in a leaded framework so as to form a kind of mosaic, upon which contours, features and folds of drapery were painted in line.   But it now became the practice to paint the whole design on large sheets of uncoloured glass ; the process was thus essentially the same as that employed by the enameller of a glass vessel, or for that matter, by the painter of maiolica, though the colours were generally thinner, in order that the passage of the light might not be unduly hindered. It is easy to imagine that changes of this kind in the art of orna-menting a glass base might suggest similar modifications to a kindred art like that of the enameller on metal[1].

As in the case of translucent enamel on sunk relief, the question of precedence between France and North Italy is by no means easy to decide.   If any part of the decoration of enamels in the round, like the Rössl of Altötting (see above, p. 58), can be fairly described as painted enamel, then the French claim is a strong one; and it is confirmed if the small enamelled copper plaques, probably made at Limoges and now respectively preserved in the Musée des Antiquaires de L'Ouest at Poitiers, and the Musée Vivenel at Compiègne, are really of the period of Charles VII, as the cos-tumes of the personages upon them appear to indicate.   On the other hand, it must be noted that the well-known artist Jehan Foucquet, who used to insert little medallions of enamel, painted in the Italian style, in the frames of his pictures[2], was the friend of

[1] See M. Molinier's article on the beginnings of painted enamelling, in *Gazette des Beaux-Arts*, 3rd period, XXIV, 1900, p. 422 f.

[2] The ground of the enamels of Foucquet and Filarete was black, on which the designs were painted in gold.   Foucquet's two surviving medallions are described by J. J. Marquet de Vasselot, *Deux émaux de Jehan Foucquet*, in *Gazette des Beaux-Arts*, August, 1904: they are in the Louvre, and in the Kunstgewerbe Museum at Berlin. See also O. von Falke, as above, p. 892, who suggests that neither France nor Italy but Flanders, the country of the monkey beaker mentioned below, may have first employed the new method.

Filarete in Italy; and that Filarete, as we know from his *Commentaries*, was in his turn a friend of the Venetian glass-maker Beroviero. The reproduction by this sculptor of the statue of Marcus Aurelius on the Capitol at Rome, a work now in the Dresden Museum and dated A.D. 1465, has diminutive plaques of painted enamel. Moreover, Venice would be quite a likely place for the invention of the new process. Once more we are confronted with a problem which admits of no certain answer. We can only say that painted enamelling appeared both in France and Italy towards the middle of the fifteenth century, and that whether the invention was independently made, or whether one country borrowed from the other, the style and system of production remain in each case distinct. In France the new method was rapidly employed upon an industrial scale; and as in earlier centuries, Limoges established a large market for her enamels. In Italy there was no such commercial manufacture. The work was confined to paxes, medallions, diptychs, triptychs, enseignes for hats and other plaques of small size: the artists, who were evidently influenced by the painters of the North Italian schools, seem to have lived in different cities and to have worked for a few patrons rather than for the general public. Their production hardly lasted for more than a single generation, and had come to an end at an early period in the sixteenth century. The drawing is usually restrained and severe; the flesh is painted in grisaille, finely shaded but never coloured; the background is often of translucent enamel, sometimes of brilliant colour, as in the fine portrait medallions in the British Museum, where it is of a rich crimson. Of less artistic importance, though highly decorative in effect, are the contemporary enamelled ciboria for church use, plateaux, candlesticks, trenchers and other domestic objects, made in considerable numbers at Venice, and illustrated by a ciborium in the McClean Bequest (no. 75). The ground is here generally a rich deep blue on which the gadroons or other modelled features stand out effectively in white, the whole being finally picked out with gold. A ciborium of this class in a French collection is signed *Bernardinus de Caramellis Plebanus fecit fieri de anno MCCCCCII*[1].

---

[1] *Gazette des Beaux-Arts*, 2nd period, XX, p. 59.

The "monkey beaker" formerly in the collections of Lord
Arundel of Wardour and of Herr Thewalt, now in that of
Mr Pierpont Morgan[1], is painted in grisaille and gold on a black
ground; it was probably made in the Low Countries in the latter
part of the fifteenth century. The beakers at Vienna, including
the Pokal of the Emperor Frederick III and the Werdenberg'scher
Pokal[2], have a ground inlaid with small stars and rays in gold, the
general appearance being very similar to that of the Venetian
work, where however the effect is usually produced by gilding the
surface. It is considered probable that the art of the two areas
must be related, and that the one centre must have influenced the
other; but it is uncertain through what channels the influence was
exerted.

The enamellers of Limoges did not, like the Italians, find
models among the works of native artists; they sought them
abroad, at first in Flanders and Germany, and after the first
quarter of the sixteenth century, in Italy. In the works of the
earlier masters the influence of German and Flemish prints is
unmistakeable, while in some cases the composition appears to
be related to that of Flemish tapestries. The artists who furnished
the models were still in great measure faithful to mediaeval tradition: the canopies under which the figures often stand illustrate
the compromises attempted by the architects of the time of
Louis XII between classical forms and those of fifteenth-century
Gothic. But by the middle of the sixteenth century all eyes were
turned to Italy, and engravings after Raphael and his school by
Marcantonio, the master of the Die, and others, were reproduced,
with an almost tedious fidelity, from which only a man of genius
like Jean Penicaud was able to emancipate his art. Subjects like
the Banquet of the Gods, the Story of Cupid and Psyche, and
other episodes based upon pagan legend, sink by constant repetition to the mediocrity of the most popular devotional subjects.

We may assign the painted enamels of Limoges to four periods:
the early or primitive; the fine period; the decline; and the last

[1] O. von Falke, as above, p. 893; Lewis Day, *Enamelling*, p. 163.

[2] J. von Schlosser, *Album ausgewählter Gegenstände der...Sammlung des allerhöchsten
Kaiserhauses*, Vienna, 1901, pls. vii and viii. These beakers may be Austrian imitations
of Flemish work (see von Falke, as above, p. 894).

final phase of decadence. The first period lasted from the beginning of the art, towards the middle of the fifteenth century, down to about 1530; the second from this date to about 1580; the third to about 1625; and the fourth to the closing of the workshops in the eighteenth century.

The first of the enamellers known to us by at least a provisional name is "Monvaerni[1]" who flourished about the middle of the fifteenth century. An artist of considerable power, though unequal both in his drawing and his colour, he conveys his meaning with an intense sincerity, making no attempt to captivate the eye by prettiness or soft refinements of execution. His enamel is thickly applied, and his figures are outlined in black, a feature which recalls the technique of the painter on glass. He has a taste for white draperies, and his favourite flesh-tint is a pearly grey. A vivid yellow and green are conspicuous in his scale of colour. His work is best studied in the Louvre; but remarkable examples have passed into the hands of American collectors. A more familiar name is that of Nardon (Léonard) Penicaud, born about A.D. 1474, and still alive in 1539. His principal activity thus falls in the period of Gothic tradition and northern models, though he lived to see the triumph of Italian influence. He works *sur apprêt*, that is to say, upon a white ground: over this he applies translucent colours which are singularly rich and sumptuous, the effect being enhanced by a free use of gold and of small "jewelled" borders enriched with little discs of foil beneath the glaze (*paillons*).

---

[1] J. J. Marquet de Vasselot, *Burlington Magazine*, October 1908, pp. 30 ff., *Revue Archéologique*, March-April 1911, pp. 299 ff., and *Gazette des Beaux-Arts*, 1910, *Les émaux de Monvaerni au Musée du Louvre*. A. Darcel, *Gazette des Beaux-Arts*, 2nd period, XIX, p. 522 f., and 3rd period, I, 1889, p. 256; E. Molinier, *ibid.*, 3rd period, XXIV, 1900, p. 426; G. Migeon, *Les Arts*, 1906, p. 24. The existence of an artist of so peculiar a name as Monvaerni is doubted, though the word, or part of it, occurs on a triptych formerly in the Odiot Collection, and on an enamel in the possession of the Countess Dzyalinska at Cracow (*Les Arts*, as above, p. 24). Mr H. P. Mitchell (*Burlington Magazine*, April, 1910, pp. 37 ff.) has suggested that the word conceals the name and title of Jean Barton de Montbas, Archbishop of Nazareth, who had been bishop of Limoges, A.D. 1458—1484, in which case the name would be that of a patron and not that of an artist: the hypothesis has however been adversely criticised. All that can at present be said is that the artist of this group of enamels was a man of marked personality and great talent, but that his identity remains obscure.

His flesh-tints are remarkable for a violet tint, which is sometimes unpleasingly dark, and rich browns are conspicuous in his scheme of colour.   A number of enamellers imitated his style, to one of whom may be assigned the small medallion in the McClean Bequest (no. 63).

To the fifty years of the next or fine period belong most of the great enamellers, of whom we may specially mention the three Jean Penicauds, and the artist allied to their school who sometimes signs K. I. P.; Léonard Limousin; Pierre Reymond; and Couly Nouailher (Noylier).   The Penicaud family had a large atelier, the products of which are commonly marked on the back with a monogrammatic stamp, but the presence of this stamp does not necessarily imply that the whole enamel is the work of one of the Penicauds, any more than the signature of a painter is always a proof that the whole of a painting is by his own hand.   Much of the less important detail was doubtless executed by pupils, the master carrying out the important features; in other cases the whole is the work of inferior artists.

Jean Penicaud I, perhaps a nephew of Nardon, is a transitional artist still working *sur apprêt*, and employing an equally sumptuous scale of colour.   He uses paillons freely, but not, like his predecessors, chiefly in the orfreys or borders of garments.   His compositions, like those of Monvaerni, recall the designs of Flemish tapestries[1].

With Jean Penicaud II, brother or cousin of the last, the process *sur apprêt* is abandoned, and painting in *grisaille* or *camaïeu* on dark blue or black ground becomes popular[2].   This artist was a master of technique, and attempted very subtle effects, especially in his treatment of faces and of the nude.   His son, Jean Penicaud III, was the greatest of the name, a real artist who designed many of his own compositions, and emancipated himself from the servile reproduction of foreign models.   K. I. P., an artist who produced small enamelled plaques with cavalry encounters and similar scenes, executed with great vigour, was evidently

---

[1] *Gazette des Beaux-Arts*, 3rd period, XXIV, 1900, p. 428.

[2] For descriptions of the process of painting in grisaille see Darcel, *Gazette des Beaux-Arts*, 2nd period, XIX, 1865, p. 528.

associated with the Penicaud atelier. Some have even identified him with Jean Penicaud II[1].

Léonard Limousin[2], perhaps the most celebrated of all enamellers, was at his best about the middle of the sixteenth century; by 1570 his work had degenerated, and his death occurred within ten years of that date. He never had so fine a taste or such prodigious powers of execution as the Penicauds, but his scope was wider, and his official position as *peintre du roi* gave him a distinction in his own day which has survived to our own. He painted groups and ornamental designs both in colour and in grisaille, but is chiefly known for his portraits, which have come down to us in considerable numbers. Some of these are admirable works; yet as a class they lack breadth and freedom: they are too faithful in their imitation of the contemporary school of French art; and this often lends them a certain provincial air. The grounds are blue or black; the shading of the features and the rendering of the hair are of the most minute and careful execution. The subjects include many of the most notable personages of the French Court.

In his grisailles, Léonard sometimes substituted a turquoise blue for the more common black ground: in his coloured work he uses foils under brilliant translucent colours heightened with gold. In one phase of his art he affected white grounds, and avoided deep and opaque colours, a manner in which he was followed by inferior artists. The panel in the McClean Collection (no. 68) is executed in this manner and is by an enameller influenced by this style.

Pierre Reymond[3] enjoyed a long career, during which he produced a great number of dishes, tazzas and other objects, now distributed among the museums and private collections of Europe. He signed pieces as early as 1538, was still working in 1570, and

---

[1] A plaque with a figure of Dialectic shows, upon the pedestal on which Dialectic sits, a combat of cavalry in K. I. P.'s characteristic style. But one of the three other plaques of the same set is signed by Jean Penicaud, and has the stamp of the atelier on the back (*Gaz. des Beaux-Arts*, 2nd period, XXXIII, 1886, p. 130). A panel in the British Museum representing St Mary of Egypt is also signed I. P. Mr H. P. Mitchell has suggested an identification with Jean Poillevé (*Burlington Magazine*, 1909, pp. 278 ff.).

[2] Signature L. L.

[3] Signature P. R.

died in 1584, but the period of his highest achievement was the middle of the century. He is chiefly noted for his grisailles, which are somewhat hard in style and are monotonous when seen in numbers. The flesh-tints have a pronounced salmon tint, and shading with hatched black lines is carried to excess, producing a too obvious resemblance to engraving. Productive as Pierre Reymond was, much of the work that bears his name must have been done by his apprentices, for like the Penicauds he had a large atelier: Martin Didier[1], an enameller who affects a strong contrast of whites and profound blacks, belongs to Reymond's school. Pierre Courtois, or Courteys[2], who worked both in colour and grisaille, is the artist of the medallions executed for the Château de Madrid now in the Louvre: they are remarkable as among the largest enamels made at Limoges.

One other artist of the best period may be mentioned here, the first of another family which was long represented through the later years of decadence—Couly Nouailher or Noylier[3], whose best work falls between 1539 and 1545. His grisailles are often poor in execution and somewhat archaistic in style. He is fond of subjects representing persons in contemporary costume, often accompanied by inscriptions which degenerate into a patois; and both the salt-cellar (no. 66) and the panels with illustrations to the clauses of the Lord's Prayer (see no. 67) are ascribed to him. The attribution is confirmed by the signature C. N. with the date 1545 on a casket of similar style in the Musée de l'Hôtel Pincé at Angers[4]; but some panels in the style are so poor, that one would prefer to believe them the work of apprentices in the master's workshop. It would be interesting to learn the name of the enameller MP, to whom the Adoration of the Magi (no. 64) and its two parallels in Paris are ascribed; but the identification has not yet been made.

[1] Signature M. D.

[2] Signature P. C. The Courtois family, like that of the Penicauds, Reymonds and Nouailhers and Laudins, gave other members to the craft. Jean Courtois, who signs I. C., exaggerates the rendering of muslin and parades his knowledge of anatomy. His flesh-tints are even brighter than those of Pierre Reymond.

[3] Signature C. N. Couly is a form of Nicolas, as Nardon of Léonard.

[4] L. Gonse, *Chefs d'œuvres des Musées de France: sculptures, dessins, objets d'art,* p. 53, Paris, 1904.

To the period of decline belong many members of the families of Limousin, Court, de Court, and Courtois, whose relationships and identities are difficult to disentangle. Jean and François Limousin belong to the family of Léonard[1]. The former, who has a preference for green grounds and brown costumes enriched with foils, flourished at the close of the century. His work is often of no inconsiderable merit. His contemporary Jean Courtois, or Courteys, deserves favourable notice as a colourist[2].

Jean de Court, and above all Suzanne de Court, illustrate this period at its climax. They abandon the discreeter harmonies of the earlier masters, cover the surface with bright greens and blues enhanced to excess by an abundant use of foil, and sacrifice all to a rich and variegated effect. Though the flesh-tints employed by Suzanne de Court are of too dead a white, and her characteristic faces *au museau pointu* are too abnormal to please, yet the general effect of her work is highly decorative; it may be well studied in the fine examples in the Waddesdon Bequest in the British Museum.

The period of decadence, chiefly represented by works of the seventeenth century, can show no artist of more than average merit, while most are little more than journeymen, without any claim to originality or power. There is neither grace nor life in their designs, which are purely imitative, and even in the case of the better men, seldom rise above the level of mediocrity. In this period the art was chiefly in the hands of the Nouailhers and the Laudins, though at the beginning of the century H. Poncet produced grisailles of respectable quality. Painted enamelling was really dead at the end of the seventeenth century; and though Jean Laudin even at that late hour attempted to galvanise it into life, his efforts remained without durable results. This artist, however, deserves mention, for though his drawing is without life, it is generally correct, a merit which is almost excellence at a time when the ateliers were turning out either devotional panels with sacred subjects and figures of saints devoid of all artistic qualities, or little

[1] Jean signs I. L. or I. + L.
[2] Examples of this artist's work in the Waddesdon Bequest in the British Museum show such affinities, especially in the turquoise colour and characteristic treatment of the trees, to the McClean pax, no. 69.

plaques of trivial appearance intended for the decoration of purses
and other objects of secular use. Among the more popular products of the time were shallow lobed cups with two handles (no. 71),
the sides painted with floral designs, the central medallions with
cupids or other figure-subjects. The ground is often white, painted
with tulip-like flowers in orange-yellow, a style which is of interest
from its resemblance to contemporary Russian work. The simi-
larity is explained by the tradition that the art of painting in
enamel was introduced into Russia by a member of the Laudin
family.

The colour scheme at this time is less rich and harmonious than
in the earlier periods; the orange-reds and yellows which often
positively offend the eye are very extensively employed. The
enamellers appear to have used the brush in applying their colours
to a greater extent than their predecessors, who, as already remarked, relied almost entirely upon the spatula and the point.

In the seventeenth and eighteenth centuries the art was practised
in Germany as well as in France, but the work was usually upon a
small scale and of no particular merit. The introduction in Paris
about A.D. 1630 by the Toutin family of fine enamel painting on a
small scale upon a white ground, led to the production of the
enamelled miniatures to which Petitot gave so great a vogue in
the reign of Louis XIV[1]. In Germany small oval and circular
plaques with landscapes and figure subjects and floral designs on a
white ground were freely used to decorate furniture and objects of
domestic use in the latter part of the seventeenth century. As in
the case of translucent champlevé enamels, Augsburg appears to
have been the principal centre; in this city the tradition of enamelling was preserved for a long series of years, for as we have already
seen, it was noted for its translucent enamels on the precious metals
from the second half of the sixteenth century. The enamelling of
watch cases, especially in France and Holland, illustrates the same
fashion; the way was thus prepared for the enamelled tabatières
and bonbonnières, to the decoration of which the art of Léonard
Limousin had sunk by the close of the eighteenth century. In our

[1] H. H. Cunynghame, *European Enamels*, ch. viii. The enamelling of miniatures
s also discussed by Mr Alexander Fisher in the work quoted at the beginning of this
section.

own country, where the enamelled miniature portrait survived in the meritorious works of Henry Bone, R.A., and the less excellent panels of Craft, the enamelled trinkets of Paris were imitated with success at Battersea, though the copies never attained the grace of the better French models.

It is impossible in the present place to enter upon the wide subject of oriental enamels. It has already been mentioned that Chinese, and therefore Japanese, cloisonné enamelling is probably to be ascribed to western inspiration; a similar origin is inferred in the case of the earlier Saracenic enamels (see p. 44). The Persian painted enamels of the seventeenth and eighteenth centuries are in like manner developments of the western process. It may be assumed that India derived her knowledge of the enameller's art from Persia, and therefore that the brilliant enamels produced in many parts of Hindustan, but notably at Jaipur, are indirectly at least of western descent.

Although ancient niello is not represented in the Collection, it may be of interest to add a few words upon its use in the arts, since it is employed in a somewhat similar manner to enamel.

Niello is not vitreous but metallic: its principal constituents are silver, lead, sulphur and copper; but the proportions of each have varied at different periods[1], so that substances of different composition may all be classed under the generic name. In the most ancient examples of its use, which date from the eighteenth Egyptian dynasty[2], copper appears to predominate over silver, while in later times, for instance in the recipe given by Theophilus, the contrary was sometimes the case. But whatever the composition, niello fuses at a much lower temperature than enamel, and is therefore easier to employ. As if in compensation for this, it is also softer, and is therefore more easily disintegrated.

[1] See the tables given by Dr Marc Rosenberg, *Geschichte der Goldschmiedekunst auf technischer Grundlage, Abteilung Niello*, 1907, a work to which the student may be referred for a comprehensive treatment of the subject. The word is derived from *nigellum*, on account of its blackness, the dark tint contrasting effectively with the colour of the metal (gold, silver, bronze, &c.) in which it is inlaid.

[2] It is not finally decided whether the Egyptian substance is to be defined as niello, but it is clearly metallic and not vitreous. The objects in which it occurs are the axe and dagger of King Ahmose, and a gold hawk's head from the tomb of Queen Ah-hetep, his mother (von Bissing, *Ein Thebanischer Grabfund*, 1900; Rosenberg, as above, p. 3).

Between the Egyptian metallic inlay and the next examples in point of time, there is an interval of many centuries. The Greeks appear to have used niello little, if at all, and it is not until Roman times that it becomes common[1]. Roman examples are abundant both on silver and other metals; and the niello designs upon silver plate are often exceedingly effective. Byzantine art continued the Roman tradition: the silver dishes found in Russia and in Cyprus[2] give evidence of considerable skill and taste; while gold finger-rings and other small objects receive the same kind of ornament[3].

Niello was much used in the West in the early Middle Ages, especially by the Anglo-Saxons[4], but the period of its greatest popularity lies between the years 1100 and 1200, when fine examples like the portable altar at Paderborn, the Reliquary of St Victor at Xanten, and the cross of St Trudpert were made[5]. It was employed in the Mohammedan world in the eleventh century[6], and a silver amulet at Stockholm of that date shows characteristics which must probably be attributed to oriental influences passing northwards through Russia, a country where early mediaeval niello is also found[7]. Although at the beginning of the thirteenth century the famous monastic goldsmith Frère Hugo of Oignies[8] employed niello to a considerable extent and it was popular with the jewellers of the century following, it declined in favour in the later Gothic period, to revive in Italy and Flanders during the Renaissance. It would be profitless to linger over the well-known

---

[1] A remarkable copper ewer and basin in the Museum at Budapest, which are of the Ptolemaic period, 2nd century B.C., have figures outlined in gold upon a background of a black material which certainly appears to be niello, although this has been disputed.

[2] For references see British Museum *Catalogue of Early Christian and Byzantine Antiquities*, nos. 376—424; *Archaeologia*, Vols. LVII and LX.

[3] *Catalogue*, as above, nos. 121 ff., 284, &c.

[4] Ring of Ethelwulf and other objects in the Gold Ornament Room in the British Museum.

[5] Rosenberg, as above, figs. 16 ff.

[6] G. Migeon, *Manuel d'art Musulman*, II, 1907, p. 150.

[7] *Collection Khanenko* (Kieff, 1902, Livraison V).

[8] A crozier by Frère Hugo is in the British Museum. Among the objects from his hand preserved by the Sœurs de Notre Dame at Namur is a book-cover finely ornamented with niello (*Gazette des Beaux-Arts*, 2nd period, XXII, 1880, p. 337). P. Kristeller, *Jahrbuch der königlich preussischen Kunstsammlungen*, Vol. XV, pp. 94 ff. Later Flemish work is represented by a fine nielloed cup in the British Museum.

discussions on the connection of the Italian nielloed paxes and other objects with the discovery of the art of engraving upon metal. It need only be said that although the art of the niello-worker is no longer considered to possess the significance once attributed to it in this regard[1], the name of Finiguerra has not quite lost its old importance for the history of engraving[2].

Painting under glass

(VERRE ÉGLOMISÉ)

THE art of decorating glass by designs etched in gold or silver foil is of considerable antiquity, the oldest known examples going back at least to the first century of our era. In most of these early specimens colour was either altogether omitted or applied very sparingly: it did not begin to predominate before the later Middle Ages, but in the pictures of the seventeenth and eighteenth centuries it occupies the whole of the surface to be decorated.

The British Museum possesses two glass bowls found at Canosa (Canusium) and ornamented with fine acanthus designs in gold foil[3]. The lower or hemispherical parts of these bowls, which alone are decorated, are double, the gold being applied to the exterior of the vessel proper, which was finally covered by an outer protective glass of the same form fitting closely over it like a cap[4]. The foil was first fixed by means of a gum; the decoration was then traced upon it, and all the gold which lay beyond the design was removed; finally, the interior details were etched in with a sharp point. The Canosa bowls, as Mr Dillon has well remarked[5],

---

[1] Rosenberg, as above, pp. 23 ff.

[2] Sir Sidney Colvin, *A Florentine picture chronicle*, &c., London, 1898, p. 30.

[3] *Archaeological Journal*, LVIII, 1901, pl. v, p. 248.

[4] In these bowls it is difficult to find any definite traces of fusion : in each the two parts are fitted together with admirable precision, the projecting edge of the inner vessel having been carefully ground down at the line of junction.

[5] *Glass*, p. 45 (The Connoisseur's Library, Methuen, 1907). It is interesting to notice that painting under glass seems to have been anticipated in very early times by painting under crystal. Dr Arthur Evans found in the smaller palace at Knossos a rock crystal plaque with traces of a building upon the back (*The Times*, August 27, 1908). The date of the palace is not later than the 17th century B.C.

reflect in character and feeling the art of an earlier period than the first century: the design has all the grace of Hellenistic ornament, and it is probable that they were actually made in Alexandria. Canusium was a city which preserved the Greek language and culture to a late period, and remained in close contact with the Greek artistic and industrial centres. It was indeed through the cities of Apulia, and through Cumae on the other side of the peninsula, that the products of the glass-maker's art first penetrated into Italy. A glass disc from Cyprus, also in the British Museum, and of similar date, has a figure of Cupid in gold foil. It probably once had a protecting glass and formed the lid of a cup or unguent pot[1].

The same process was retained by the less skilful makers of the well-known "gilded glasses" or *fondi d'oro* discovered for the most part in the Roman catacombs and dating from the period between the third and sixth centuries[2]. These are the bottoms of shallow bowls or cups, from which the sides have in almost every case been broken away, leaving flat circular medallions with ragged edges. Only the bottoms of the bowls appear to have been ornamented, the sides, if we may judge from the very rare examples preserved intact, were left perfectly plain. The *fondi d' oro* were found imbedded in the mortar with which the slabs or tiles closing the *loculi* or wall-tombs were sealed[3]; and it is supposed that at the time of the interment they were fixed by the relatives and friends of the deceased in the mortar, while it was still in a plastic condition, that they might serve as a memorial, and at the same time facilitate the identification of the tomb. The subjects are

---

[1] *Archaeological Journal*, as above, p. 247 and plate.

[2] The fullest account of these glasses will be found in Dr Hermann Vopel's *Die altchristlichen Goldgläser*, Freiburg, &c., 1899 (in Ficker's *Archäologische Studien zum Christlichen Alterthum und Mittelalter*), where references to the earlier literature are given. An account in English, chiefly based upon this monograph, will be found in the *Archaeological Journal*, 1901, pp. 225 ff. A large number of the glasses are reproduced (in outline drawings) in R. Garrucci's *Vetri ornati di figure in oro*, Rome, 1858 and 1864, as well as in the same author's *Storia dell' arte Cristiana*, Vol. III. The fine series in the British Museum are described in the Museum *Catalogue of Early Christian and Byzantine Antiquities*, 1900, nos. 598 ff.

[3] A few have been found with interments in other cities, especially in Cologne and its neighbourhood. Others have come to light at Ostia, Castel Gandolfo, &c., as well as in Egypt.

mostly portraits of husbands and wives, alone or with their children, and representations of saints; both classes are commonly accompanied by inscriptions giving their names; and acclamations such as *pie zeses* are especially frequent. The figures stand out upon the background of plain or coloured glass; the features and folds of drapery are traced with a point as in the earlier pagan examples. The addition of colour is very exceptional; as a rule it is only used to suggest jewellery, or to render the *clavi* upon garments. But in the very remarkable dish found at Cologne, now in the British Museum[1], colour was freely employed; and this object, which some have regarded as a paten, anticipates the processes which found favour in later centuries.

These methods of decorating glass may have been abandoned between the sixth and tenth centuries, but if so, the tradition at any rate was kept alive, for Heraclius, the mediaeval writer on the industrial arts, who lived in the tenth century, was familiar with all its details, and describes experiments which he made himself[2]. Theophilus, another mediaeval writer on the arts, living about A.D. 1100, describes the method of making the glass cubes of which the gold background of Byzantine mosaics was composed[3]; he asserts that the "Greeks" decorated glass cups with gold, and the glass vessels from Constantinople in the Treasury of St Mark's at Venice show that there is nothing improbable in the statement. Jean de Garlande (fl. 11—13th century) also mentioned glass vessels with gold ornament; and Cennino Cennini, the Paduan artist, writing at the end of the fourteenth century, describes how

---

[1] *Catalogue of Early Christian and Byzantine Antiquities*, no. 628; this object is so damaged and decayed that it does not admit of successful reproduction by photography. A figure is given in Nesbitt's *Catalogue of the Slade Collection*, p. 50. See also *Bonner Jahrbücher*, XLII, 1867, pl. v; Garrucci, *Storia*, &c., pl. 169, fig. 1.

[2] Heraclius, *De coloribus et artibus Romanorum* (trs. by Mrs Merrifield, 1849), I, ch. v; A. Ilg's edition is in R. Eitelberger von Edelberg's *Quellenschriften für Kunstgeschichte...des Mittelalters*, Vol. IV, Vienna, 1873.

[3] *Diversarum artium Schedula*, II, 15; R. Hendrie's edition, London, 1847; A. Ilg's edition in *Quellenschriften*, as above, VII, 1874. Theophilus appears to have been a German who had visited Sicily. The long-accepted tradition which identified him with Rugerus or Rogkerus seems to rest upon insufficient evidence (Marc Rosenberg, *Geschichte der Goldschmiedekunst: Abteilung Niello*). Theophilus describes the manufacture by "the Greeks" of the gilded cubes of glass used as backgrounds in Byzantine mosaics. Gold leaf was applied to one surface, and a film of glass blown over it as a protection.

to decorate with designs in gold panels for caskets and reliquaries[1]. Cennini makes no mention of a second protecting glass, which seems to have been now generally abandoned.

There remain several interesting examples of glass etched with a point upon gold leaf, and with added colour, belonging to a period earlier than Cennini. It was evidently quite a usual thing to inlay plaques of this kind in the panels of pulpits, altar frontals and other pieces of church furniture, during the twelfth, thirteenth and fourteenth centuries[2]. A portable altar in the Victoria and Albert Museum is an early instance; but the most remarkable example in England is the old retable from the high altar of Westminster Abbey[3], now preserved in the Jerusalem Chamber. This retable is enriched with a number of small blue and purple glass plaques, to the back of which silver foil has been applied, while the front is ornamented with animal and floral designs. These are believed to have been painted on with a mixture of red ochre, wax, turpentine and linseed oil, a composition which gives them a definite relief. While the substance was still moist, gold foil was laid over it and this was easily removed when dry, from those parts of the surface not intended to be covered by the design[4]. The external decoration throws a shadow upon the silver foil of the reverse, and this enhances the effect of the whole. Such work might almost be taken for enamel by inexperienced eyes, and it was perhaps for this reason that a clause in the statutes of the Paris enamellers in A.D 1309 forbade its use except for certain articles of church furniture[5]. M. André, who has restored many early glass pictures, is of opinion that in the majority of cases, where both gold and colour were employed, the glass was first covered with foil applied by means of gum. On such parts as were to have only gold, any required pattern was traced with a point, while from those which were to be

---

[1] *Il libro dell' arte o trattato della pittura.* Italian edition, Florence, 1859. English translation by Christina Herringham ; *The book of the art of Cennino Cennini,* London, 1899.

[2] Mr Dillon (*Glass,* p. 141) mentions examples of this work in the Romanesque churches of Apulia, notably on the pulpit at Bitonto.

[3] *Ibid.*

[4] Viollet le Duc, *Dictionnaire du Mobilier français,* p. 388. E. Dillon, *Glass,* as above.

[5] *La Collection Spitzer,* Vol. II, p. 57.

painted the gold was entirely removed, and after the whole had been cleaned, the high lights and flesh-tints were first painted in, then the other colours in successive applications, with the addition of fine silver foil here and there to produce a richer effect[1]. In small plaques without figures the design was often reserved in the gold foil while the whole ground was painted crimson, green or black. The back may be protected by a varnish, but it is very seldom that there is a second protecting glass.

The best fourteenth and fifteenth century examples appear to come chiefly from the North of Italy, and it may be conjectured that Venice and Milan were the principal centres of production. The splendid example in the McClean Bequest (no. 76) is certainly of Italian origin, and is probably of the fourteenth century. The fine collection bequeathed by the Marquis Emmànuele d'Azeglio to the Museo Civico at Turin contains early examples among numerous specimens of later date; others are in the British and Victoria and Albert Museums[2]. Glass pictures continued popular through the period of the Renaissance, colour gradually predominating over gold. In the sixteenth century the process was applied to crystal jewels, and to the central medallions of Venetian glass dishes[3]. But larger panels with figure subjects were still produced, and were popular north of the Alps: a panel in the Salting Collection is assigned to Germany; and the plaque in the present Bequest representing St Jerome (no. 77) may also be of German origin. Plaques of painted glass were inlaid in the elaborate cabinets which were fashionable in Germany in the seventeenth century. The succeeding century saw no diminution in the popularity of the art. The attractive plaque (no. 78) representing the Virgin and Child seems to be a work of its earlier years, and is evidently based upon a picture by a master of the eclectic school of Bologna. As the century advanced, the work tended to become coarser: several very

---

[1] *Ibid.* p. 58.

[2] Those in the British Museum are not specially remarkable. For the examples in the Victoria and Albert Museum see *Archaeological Journal*, 1901, p. 250. A fine 14th-century example with the Crucifixion is in the Church of the Holy Cross at Rostock (*Zeitschrift für Christliche Kunst*, 1895, pp. 278 ff.).

[3] Examples in the great Museums. A remarkably fine specimen is in the Dutuit Collection in the Petit Palais, Paris. Such dishes continued to be made in the 17th century.

rough examples assigned to Venice are in the Victoria and Albert
Museum, together with an English portrait of a lady. The last
and worst phase of the art was reached when inferior mezzotints
were stuck to the glass, scraped so thin as to be quite transparent,
and finally coarsely coloured, from the back. Such pictures are
still frequently to be seen in cottages and in the curiosity shops in
English towns.

It was in the eighteenth century that the term *Verre églomisé*
was first used to describe painting under glass, and since it has
firmly established itself in the language of the sale room and the
catalogue, it may be well to explain its origin[1]. A certain
M. Glomy, calling himself *dessinateur*, but largely occupied with
the framing of pictures, lived at the corner of the rue de Bourbon
and the rue Saint-Claude at Paris. He was especially known for
the pictures painted on glass which he framed and sold: they
became so fashionable and were so widely distributed that the
word *églomiser* was coined to describe them. M. Darcel drew
attention to a passage in *L'Intermédiaire*[2] which proved that the
word soon travelled as far as Lyon. Now it was precisely at Lyon
that M. Carrand the elder first printed the word in a catalogue of
paintings under glass published about 1825. Henceforward its
fortune was made; it was generally adopted by collectors, and
found its way into the catalogue of the Musée de Cluny: the
Italians also incorporated it into their language, giving it the
form *Vetro agglomizzato*. In this disguise its pedigree would be
difficult indeed to trace: it has a certain fine archaic sound,
suggesting an old descent and an intrinsic meaning. Like many
other unsatisfactory terms which have the merit of brevity it is
retained as a matter of convenience, and the efforts to dislodge it
have hitherto been unsuccessful. And it must be admitted that
églomiser has the same position in the French language as the
word macadamise in our own.

[1] The information given above is derived from an article by M. Bonnaffé in the
Chronique des Arts, 1884, the substance of which is reproduced in *La Collection Spitzer*,
II, pp. 54 ff.

[2] Vol. XIV, col. 514. "J'ai une aquarelle sous verre, qui est entourée d'un encadre-
ment noir brodé de filets d'or. Ces filets ont été peints à l'envers du verre, ainsi que la
bande noire...il y a au bas, écrit à la pointe sèche dans le noir: 'églomisé par Hoeth à
Lyon.'"

Such are a few of the points to which an examination of the more important divisions of the McClean Bequest, the jewellery, the ivory carvings, the enamels, and the glass paintings, may attract the student's notice. It has long been a matter for regret that there were few such objects in the Fitzwilliam Museum, and that the opportunity of awakening an interest in the minor arts of mediaeval times was lost through the absence of actual examples. The McClean Bequest has done much to make good the deficiency; a study of its contents should help all who feel a sympathy with the artistic aims of the Middle Ages to appreciate in a higher degree the great collections in London and in the cities of continental Europe; it should add a richer colour and a greater wealth of detail to their mental pictures of mediaeval history, and introduce them to fields of research perhaps too little frequented by British scholars.

CATALOGUE

JEWELLERY AND ENGRAVED GEMS.

1. GOLD PENANNULAR ARMLET, with expanding ends.

Plate I. Prehistoric.

W. $2\frac{9}{16}$ in. The armlet dates from the latter part of the bronze age. A series of examples of this form in the British Museum were found in 1906 and 1907 at Bexley, near Dartford, Kent.

2. GOLD, PART OF A TORC, twisted from three wires.

Plate II. Viking period.
W. $2\frac{11}{16}$ in.

3. FIBULA, bronze gilt. It is of the "cross-bow" type, with long hollow stem, ornamented at the edges with raised pelta-like crescents, and high arched bow terminating in a knob, the cross-piece ending in similar knobs: a band of nielloed ornament runs along the middle of the bow and stem, the design consisting of alternate lozenges and rings. The pin works on a wire within the hollow cross-bar, and passes through a lateral slit in the stem.

Roman, 4th century.

L. 4·34 in.

For fibulae of this type see *Bonner Jahrbücher*, Heft 112, p. 396; Linden-schmit, *Alterthümer unserer heidnischen Vorzeit*, Vol. III, Heft II, pl. iv. The type begins towards the close of the third century and continues throughout the fourth. An interesting example with a Christian monogram, and offering many points of resemblance to that here described, is in the British Museum (*Catalogue of Early Christian and Byzantine Antiquities*, no. 256). One at Mainz, figured by Lindenschmit, as above, fig. 6, is also closely similar.

4. CIRCULAR BROOCH, the front of gold plates, the disc at the back of silver. In the centre of the front is a high boss with cruciform bars upon a base of shell or ivory: round it are four equidistant sockets once containing shell, and between these a cruciform design of garnets on concentric circles alternately of garnet and filigree. The side-edges are ornamented with cable wire and parallel sunk lines. The back has round the edge a band of zoomorphic design, and from it project the hinge and socket of a pin, both riveted and engraved with simple ornament.

Plate II. Jutish, First half of the 7th century.

D. 3⅛ in. From the King's Field, Faversham. Formerly in the Kennard Collection.

This is one of a number of fine Jutish brooches found for the most part in Kent, though a few have been found elsewhere, notable examples being two found near Abingdon in Berkshire (Akerman, *Pagan Saxondom*, pl. iii; *Archaeological Journal*, IV, p. 253; *Victoria County History, Berkshire*, Vol. I, p. 241). The finest example of all is the Kingston brooch, discovered on Kingston Down by Bryan Faussett between 1767 and 1773 (*Inventorium Sepulcrale*, pp. 35—94). Others of great beauty have been excavated at Sarre in a cemetery which yielded coins of Heraclius (d. 641), Maurice Tiberius (d. 602) and Chlotaire II (d. 628). For these see *Victoria County History, Kent*, Vol. I, pp. 357—358.

The King's Field at Faversham proved a very prolific site, and a fine series of inlaid brooches and other objects obtained there were bequeathed to the nation by Mr W. Gibbs in 1870. They are now in the British Museum.

5. GOLD DISC FOR A BROOCH, with a design of inlaid garnets forming a circle from which radiate four triangles. Within the design are stepped cloisons with eight lapis pastes symmetrically disposed. The remaining stones are garnets.

Between the triangles are four circular settings, three empty, the other containing a carbuncle. The ground is ornamented with filigree circles.

Plate III. Jutish, First half of the 7th century.
D. 1¾ in. From the King's Field, Faversham.

6. GOLD BRACTEATE, embossed with two interlaced lacertine monsters on a ground of chequers: loop for suspension.

Plate III. Jutish, First half of the 7th century.
D. 1¼ in. From the King's Field, Faversham.

A gold bracteate stamped with a star pattern was found with the Kingston Brooch (*Victoria County History, Kent*, Vol. I, pl. ii, fig. 10, opposite p. 360).

7. GOLD BRACTEATE with concentric design of stamped chequered triangles. Central setting, now empty, and raised pearled border.

Jutish, First half of the 7th century.
D. 1¼ in. From the King's Field, Faversham.

8. GOLD OPENWORK ORNAMENT in the form of a cross contained in a circle: the borders pearled throughout.

Plate I. Jutish, 7th century.
D. ¹¹⁄₁₆ in. From the King's Field, Faversham.

9. CIRCULAR BROOCH, bronze overlaid with a gold plate on which is a cruciform design enriched at the ends with four carbuncles: between the arms are ornaments of glass pastes and other materials. In the centre is a raised circular setting, now empty. The ground is covered with S-scrolls and circles, and round the edge is a cable border. At the back is an iron pin much rusted.

Plate III. Frankish, late 8th century.
D. 2 in. From the Forman Collection.

For brooches of the class represented by this and the following number see H. Baudot, *Mémoire sur les sépultures des barbares de l'époque Mérovingienne,* pls. xii—xiii; C. Boulanger, *Mobilier funéraire gallo-romain et franc,* pl. 37.

10. ANOTHER, without any disc at the back. The design is a cross formed of garnets in cells. Between them, and in the centre, are pastes (dark blue, turquoise blue, and green) in high settings. The ground is covered with filigree of a confused design.

Plate III. Frankish, late 8th century.
D. 2⅛ in. From the Forman Collection.

11. BRONZE BUCKLE. The oblong strap-plate is covered with cells all formerly containing garnets, of which many are now lost. The central panel has a square inscribed in a lozenge, at each end of which are corresponding formal designs: the whole is contained in a border of oblongs bisected by diagonal lines. On the tongue of the buckle are inlaid three garnets. The bronze of the buckle was once gilt.

> *Plate II. Frankish, early 6th century.*
> L. 4⅞ in. From the Bateman Collection.
> Cf. C. Boulanger, as above, Introduction, p. lvii, figs. 109—111, and pl. 25; A. Götze, *Gotische Schnallen*, p. 22 and pl. xiii.

ENGRAVED GEMS AND PASTES.

Note.—Left and right are considered from the point of view of the spectator.

12. CHALCEDONY; scaraboid pierced longitudinally; a winged quadruped to left.

> *Plate. Perso-Greek, 5th century* B.C.
> L. 1·02 in.

Nos. 13—24 are all of the Graeco-Roman period between the first century B.C. and the close of the second century of our era.

13. SARD (fragment); a laureated head to *r.*

> L. ·6 in.
> It is difficult to decide whether this gem is of the Augustan age or a clever eighteenth-century imitation. In either case it is a work of fine quality.
> Modern setting.

14. GARNET, cabochon; Fortuna standing to *l.* holding a cornucopia and a torch.

> *1st century* A.D.
> L. ·72 in. Modern setting.

15. NICOLO; a young Satyr standing to *r.* dandling a child and playing a pipe.

> L. ·54 in. Modern setting.

16. GREEN PASTE; a young Satyr with a goat; to *l.*, a tree.

> L. ·42 in. Modern setting.

D.   6

17.   SARD; Eros seated to *l.*; before him a bird upon the top of a cage.

1st century A.D.
L. ·24 in.
A fragment is broken from one end.   The setting is modern.

18.   NICOLO; a boar standing to *r.*

2nd—3rd century A.D.
L. ·44 in.   Modern setting.

19.   NICOLO; a gryllus.

L. ·34 in.   Modern setting.

The following are doubtful.

20.   NICOLO PASTE; head of a bearded Satyr to *r.*

L. ·36 in.   Modern setting.

21.   YELLOW SARD (fragment); a horse to *l.*

1st—2nd century A.D.
L. ·34 in.   Modern setting.

22.   PASTE; a peacock to *r.*

L. ·42 in.   Modern setting

23.   SARD; cattle and sheep.

1st—2nd century A.D.?
L. ·64 in.

24.   HELIOTROPE; Helios driving his car to *r.*: in the exergue B. F. F. S.

L. ·46 in.

GNOSTIC.

25.   CHRYSOPRASE; Chnoubis to *r.*; in the field vertical inscription in two lines XNOY | BIC.

L. ·46 in.

26. COMPOSITION? A figure with human body and animal head resembling the god Set, and wearing a loincloth to the knees, stands to *r.* To *r.* and *l.* of him is the (direct) inscription:

$$
\begin{array}{cc|c}
& \text{V G} & \wedge\ \text{Є}\ \text{P}\ \ominus \\
\text{Π}\ \text{Є}\ \text{I} & & \text{C} \\
& \Delta & \text{M}\ \text{Є}\ \text{I}\ \text{N} \\
& \text{V}\ \text{I} & \omega \\
& & \ominus\ \text{I}\ \text{B}\ \text{P} \\
& & \text{I}\ \text{N}
\end{array}
$$

L. ·76 in. Modern setting.

27. HAEMATITE.

Obverse: a standing female figure, swathed, with *l.* arm raised to the head and holding an indeterminate object in her *r.* hand. Above, three feathers? *Rev.* inscription in direct letters:

$$
\begin{array}{c}
\text{B}\ \text{Ψ} \\
\text{E}\ \text{B}\ \text{E} \\
\text{Ψ}\ \text{A}\ \text{B}\ \omega \\
\text{P}
\end{array}
$$

L. ·62 in.

28. PALE SARD; Canopic jar to *r.*; above, feathers.

L. ·56 in.
Modern setting. The authenticity of this gem is not quite certain.

29. HAEMATITE.

Male figure in long garment standing to *l.* holding a sistrum in his *r.* and a bucket in his *l.* Before him is an altar on which is seen a uraeus.

L. ·52 in. Modern setting.

SASSANIAN.

On Sassanian gems see
J. Menant, *Les pierres gravées de la Haute Asie, recherches sur la glyptique orientale;*

L. de Clercq, *Collection de Clercq : Catalogue méthodique et raisonné,* &c., Vol. II,
    1903 (plates iv—vii);
F. W. Thomas, *Journ. Royal Asiatic Society,* XIII, p. 414 ;
Paul Horn, *Mittheilungen aus den orientalischen Sammlungen der königlichen
    Museen zu Berlin,* Heft IV, 1891, and *Zeitschrift der deutschen Morgen-
    ländischen Gesellschaft,* XLIV, Leipsic, 1890, pp. 650 ff. (Collection in the
    British Museum);
G. Steindorff, *Mittheilungen,* as above (Collection in the Berlin Museum) ;
A. Furtwängler, *Antike Gemmen,* Vol. III ; and various publications by
    Mr C. W. King.
Sassanian cameos exist in some numbers.   The fine specimens in the
Cabinet des Médailles of the Bibliothèque Nationale at Paris are reproduced
by E. Babelon, *Catalogue des Camées antiques et modernes,* nos. 359 ff., Paris,
1897.

30. CHALCEDONY; Seal in form of a ring with channelled
hoop and oval bezel engraved in intaglio with a wolf-like animal
above a wild sheep (pasang).

D. 1·15 in.

This is quite a usual form of Sassanian signet, and the channelling of the
hoop is also common (cf. de Clercq, *Catalogue,* as above, pl. v, fig. 95).
Animals and monsters of various kinds are common upon the intaglio stones
of the new Persian monarchy, and numerous examples are to be seen among
the collections of great museums.

31. ANOTHER ; the bezel engraved in intaglio with a female
figure standing to right beneath a round arch.

D. 1·2 in.

Doubts have been expressed as to the genuine character of this signet, but
in view of the uncertainty attending the judgment of Sassanian stones it has
been included in the catalogue.   It is well known that falsifications are common
and that Bagdad is probably a principal centre of their manufacture (Horn,
Zeitschrift, as above, p. 677).   A female figure holding a lotus is a not infrequent
subject among Sassanian gems.   For the long plait of hair worn by such figures
see Furtwängler, as above, p. 123, and *The Treasure of the Oxus,* British
Museum, 1905, no. 103.

IVORY CARVINGS.

32 and 33. TWO PANELS, perhaps from an episcopal throne.

(1) Two bearded figures (Evangelists) in tunic and pallium
and wearing shoes open over the instep stand between columns

with Corinthian capitals surmounted by an architrave. Each holds in his left hand a book, on the cover of which is a form of the sacred Monogram, and bends the fingers of his right in a gesture signifying conversation.

Above the architrave is the scene of the Healing of the Paralytic. In the middle, the healed man in a short tunic advances to the right carrying his bed and bedding on his back, and looking back over his shoulder. Our Lord stands behind him, extending his right hand in the Latin gesture of benediction; he is youthful and beardless, and without nimbus; he is dressed in tunic and pallium with sandals, and carries a cross in his left hand. On the right, a bearded apostle, similarly clad, holds up his right hand in sign of admiration. In the background is seen a wall, with round-arched doors.

(2) In the lower part of the panel are the two remaining Evangelists almost identical with the preceding, except that the right hand of the figure to the right touches the gospel which he carries. The scene above the architrave represents Christ with the woman of Samaria at the well. On the right, the woman stands facing the well, which is in the middle. She raises her right hand in astonishment, while with her left she holds the cord by which a bucket is suspended. Our Lord advances from the left as in the companion scene but with less rapid motion. The background is as before.

Plate IV. Egypt or Syria, 6th century.
L. 13½ in. B. 5⅝ in. From the Bateman Collection.

In the 17th century these panels were in the Abbey of St Maximin at Luxemburg, and are briefly described and partly illustrated by the Jesuit Alexander Wiltheim (died c. 1694) in his manuscript work *Luciliburgensia, sive Luxemburgum Romanum*, edited and published posthumously from an 18th-century copy by Dr A. Neijen, Luxemburg, 1842, nos. 188—189, pl. l, and p. 197. Also figured by Garrucci, *Storia dell' arte cristiana*, VI, pl. 452; and in the *Catalogue of the Bateman Heirlooms*, London, Sotheby's, 1893, pl. ii. See also Westwood, *Fictile ivories*, '73, 28 and 28ᵃ, p. 49; G. Stuhlfauth, *Die altchristliche Elfenbeinplastik*, p. 119 (Heft II of J. Ficker's *Archäologische Studien zum Christlichen Alterthum und Mittelalter*, Freiburg and Leipsic, 1896); E. Molinier, *Histoire générale des arts appliqués à l'industrie*, Vol. I, *Ivoires*, p. 78.

These two panels are closely related to the ivories produced in the 6th century in the Christian East, but not yet assigned with certainty to their

particular localities. Westwood remarked their resemblance in style to the
large composite book-cover in the Bibliothèque Nationale at Paris (Garrucci,
Storia, Vol. VI, pl. 458) which is itself related to the similar book-cover at
Etchmiadzin (J. Strzygowski, *Byzantinische Denkmäler*, I, 1891, *Das Etchmiadzin
Evangeliar*), to various ivory pyxes, and to the so-called chair of Archbishop
Maximianus at Ravenna (Garrucci, as above, pl. 419 ff.). The Paris book-cover
has both the gospel scenes which ornament the upper parts of these two panels,
and so have two of the pyxes (Garrucci, pl. 438, 4 and 5); the chair has the
woman at the well (Garrucci, pl. 419, 3); and in several other ivories the
commoner subject of the healing of the paralytic occurs. The statuesque
figures on the front of the chair are of the same family as the Evangelists upon
our panels, but the nearest parallels to these are to be found on a diptych of
the same oriental origin, one leaf of which, now in the Brussels Museum, was
formerly in the Spitzer Collection (*La Collection Spitzer*, Vol. I, Paris, 1890,
Ivoires, pl. i; *Gazette Archéologique*, Vol. XIV, 1889, pl. xxii; Molinier, *Ivoires*,
p. 55; J. Destrée, *Musées Royaux des arts décoratifs et industriels, Catalogue
des ivoires*, Brussels, 1902, no. 1, pp. 1—6), the other in the treasury of the
Cathedral of Tongres (Reusens, *Éléments d'archéologie Chrétienne*, Aix-la-
Chapelle, 1885, Vol. I, p. 194, fig. 195; Rohault de Fleury, *La Messe*, Vol. VI,
pl. 437; J. Helbig, *La sculpture au pays de Liège*, 1890, p. 13; C. de Roddaz,
L'art ancien à l'exposition nationale Belge, Brussels, 1882, p. 34; Molinier,
as above, p. 55). Here St Peter and St Paul are represented in a very
similar manner, and wear the same open-fronted shoes, which are also to
be seen in the frescoes of Bawît in Egypt, dating from about the sixth
century (J. Clédat, *Mém. de l'Institut français d'archéologie orientale*, XII,
1904, pls. xxi, xxvii, xxxv). The composite book-cover from Murano now at
Ravenna (Garrucci, pl. 456), though its scene of the healing of the paralytic is
closely related from the iconographical point of view, appears to be stylistically
more remote than the ivories already mentioned, though Stuhlfauth (*Altchristliche Elfenbeinplastik*, p. 121) is of the contrary opinion : on this point the
judgment of Westwood must still command assent, though there seems no
reason to follow him in suggesting the seventh century as a possible date, for
the characteristics of the work are in no way inconsistent with the art of the
sixth. Stuhlfauth's "school of Monza," to which he would assign our panels,
with the Ravenna book-cover and most of the pyxes, is now generally considered
to have only an imaginary existence; and all the ivories which he connected
with it are held to have been really produced in the Christian East. They stand
in fact on the same footing as the other carvings already mentioned, though
some of them may have originated in a different centre. The evidence which
assigns all these ivories, however grouped, to oriental Christian art, is sufficiently
conclusive : it is supported by divergences from the Roman or Italian style, by
iconographical resemblances to mosaics, mural paintings, and manuscripts of
oriental origin or inspiration, by the use of ornamental motives native in Syria
and Egypt, and by such facts as the discovery of the characteristic Etchmiadzin
gospel-cover at Etchmiadzin, a place where it is not likely to have been imported

from the West. But precise classification within the oriental group is a matter of much uncertainty. Thus iconographical details native to Syria-Palestine appear on ivories which for other reasons should be connected with Egypt. The artistic relations between these two provinces were, however, so close about the sixth century that the process of discrimination must still be conjectural, especially in cases where the survival of a common Hellenistic sentiment influenced the treatment of figure subjects. The streams of pilgrims passing in and out of the Holy Land brought ideas with them and carried others away ; the constant commercial intercourse between Alexandria, Antioch, Ephesus and Constantinople with each other, with the western Mediterranean ports, and with the inland regions behind them, tended to a culture of which the leaven was Greek and the mass Asiatic.

We conclude that these panels were probably made in the sixth century in some metropolis of the Christian East under the influence of that persistent late-Hellenistic art which still preserved even down to the sixth century traditions of the greater Hellenic sculpture. Recent researches have made it probable that many large ivory diptychs and panels of the period between the fourth and seventh centuries are related to certain sarcophagi probably made in Antioch or Southern Anatolia, and the reliefs upon these sarcophagi in their turn have affinities with Greek sculpture of a far earlier period. (See Strzygowski, *Journal of Hellenic Studies*, 1907, p. 99.)

The type of Evangelist holding a book inscribed with a cross goes back to a type of prophet known to the Jewish art of Syria and Egypt before the beginning of our era and is found very early in the mural paintings of the catacombs (J. Wilpert, *Die Malereien der Katakomber Roms*, pls. xciv, cliii). The prophets in the illustrated fifth-century world-chronicle on papyrus now in St Petersburg are similar in appearance (*Denkschriften der k. Wiener Akademie der Wissenschaften, phil. hist. Klasse*, Vol. 1, 1904, p. 149). The curious large ears characteristic of the figures on the front of the episcopal chair at Ravenna and of that on one of the early panels at Berlin (*Königliche Museen, Beschreibung der Bildwerke, Elfenbeinbildwerke*, 1902, pl. ii) are repeated in the early art of Christian Egypt (Catalogue of the Cairo Museum, *Koptische Kunst* by J. Strzygowski, pp. 243 ff.).

34. PANEL. Christ enthroned, within an oval laurel wreath suggesting a glory: in the spandrels between the wreath and the carved border of acanthus leaves are the symbols of the Evangelists. Our Lord is youthful and beardless, with full cheeks and long curly hair falling upon his shoulders; his nimbus contains a cross upon a fluted background. He is seated upon a draped throne with a long bolster-shaped cushion but no back, holding an open book in his left hand, and raising his right in the Latin gesture of benediction: he wears tunic and pallium, and his feet are bare. The symbols of the Evangelists, which are necessarily of small size, are similar to those commonly found in work of the period, but that of St Matthew is represented as seated at a desk, and writing in a book of the Gospel. Within the laurel wreath is an interior band of foliate ornament; the background, the cross in the nimbus, and the pages of the book held by Christ have all been gilded, probably in modern times.

Plate V. Carolingian, 9th century.
L. 6 in.
B. 5¼ in. From the Barrois and Ashburnham Collections; removed from the modern cover of a Gospel of the tenth century, McClean MS. 19, probably written in N.E. France.

A. Goldschmidt in *Jahrbuch der k. preussischen Kunstsammlungen*, 1905, p. 9, fig. 4.

For the group to which this ivory belongs, see Introduction, p. 22. The date of the earliest examples has been determined by Dr Goldschmidt in the article mentioned above. A pair of ivory panels now in the Louvre (E. Molinier, *Catalogue of the Ivories*, no. 9) are so exactly described in some dedicatory verses in a Carolingian Psalter in the Hofbibliothek at Vienna that they must have once adorned its cover. These verses show that the book was presented by a King Karl to a Pope Hadrian; and though on three separate occasions a Karl and a Hadrian were contemporaries, palaeographical reasons favour the identification of the donor with Charlemagne: the scribe Dagulf, whose name is mentioned as the writer of the MS., also appears to have lived in the early Carolingian period. The ivory panels must have been made for the manuscript because the verses describe all the four scenes with which they are ornamented, and two of these, the reception by St Jerome of the message from Pope Damasus requesting him to correct the Psalter according to the Septuagint, and the subsequent undertaking of the task, are by no means common subjects. The conclusion is that both the MS. in Vienna and the ivory covers in Paris must have been finished before the year A.D. 795 in which Hadrian I died.

This argument provides a *terminus a quo* for a whole series of ivories presenting the same peculiarities of style, and justifies the attribution of the better and more characteristic examples to the close of the eighth century or the earlier part of the ninth. The inferior carvings may be distributed through the ninth and early tenth centuries; for as the manuscript style with which they are connected was of wide influence and great duration, a similar longevity may be assumed for the products of the related plastic art. Even should it be urged that the Karl and Hadrian mentioned in the dedication are not the first but either the second or third pair bearing these names we still remain within the limits of the ninth century, for Charles the Bold and Hadrian II were contemporary from A.D. 867—872, and Charles the Fat and Hadrian III in A.D. 884—885. Moreover the last pair should probably be eliminated, as

Charles the Fat was Emperor and not King during the papacy of the third Hadrian.

The ivory upon this book-cover may be more especially compared with those carvings in the group brought together by Dr Goldschmidt which offer representations of Our Lord, especially with the large panel in the Bodleian Library at Oxford (Westwood, *Fictile Ivories*, pl. vi; Didron, *Annales Archéologiques*, XX, p. 118), as to which there had previously been some uncertainty of opinion (see Introduction, p. 23). Its central figure represents Our Lord standing upon the lion and dragon; the youthful beardless face and long flowing hair are very similar, and the drapery is treated in the same manner. The resemblance to another ivory in the group is not so close, though the subject is almost identical. This is the panel in the Berlin Museum, formerly in the Davillier and Odiot Collections (Königliche Museen, *Beschreibung der Bildwerke der Christlichen Epoche*, 1902, no. 39 A, pl. 13; Westwood, *Fictile Ivories*, pl. xiii; *Gazette des Beaux-Arts*, Période III, Vol. I, 1889, p. 247; Goldschmidt, as above, fig. 11, p. 15), where Christ is also seated in glory holding a book and blessing with his right hand. Another ivory which it is instructive to compare is the great panel in five parts in the Victoria and Albert Museum (W. Maskell, *Description of the Ivories...in the South Kensington Museum*, p. 53), the companion panel to which is in the Vatican (R. Kanzler, *Gli avori dei Musei sacro e profano della Biblioteca Vaticana, Museo Sacro*, pl. iv, Rome, 1903) and has in the centre a figure of our Lord trampling upon lion and dragon, as in the Bodleian book-cover. Other examples of the group which are in England and accessible to the student are in the British Museum (*Archaeologia*, Vol. LVIII, pl. xxxiii, and fig. 3 on p. 432; H. Graeven in *Photographischer Nachbildung*, Series I, no. 31) and in the John Rylands Library at Manchester (formerly in the Bateman and Crawford Collections; South Kensington Museum photographs, no. 14220). The remaining examples, chiefly in France, Germany and Italy, are mentioned in Dr Goldschmidt's list (pp. 16—19).

The foliated borders so frequent upon Carolingian diptychs are derived from those of late classical and early Byzantine times. Such borders were commonly of palmettes or acanthus leaves, examples of the former being seen on the famous diptych of the Symmachi and Nicomachi, of which the two leaves are at South Kensington and in the Louvre respectively, and of the latter on consular diptychs and other sculptures[1]. On the fine diptych in the Liverpool Museum with Aesculapius and Hygeia, the palmette and acanthus-leaf are used alternately. Some borders were imitated from architectural mouldings, such as the egg and dart, or the astragalus. The oval foliate band within the laurel of our ivory panel is of a hybrid design which suggests a

---

[1] Panel representing Bellerophon on Pegasus in the British Museum, where the foliage is incised and not in relief; diptych of the Consul Boethius (A.D. 487) at Brescia (Molinier, *Ivoires*, no. 5, p. 19). Round the panels of the simulated marble doors in the gallery at Sta Sophia, Constantinople (*Jahrbuch der königlich preussischen Kunstsammlungen*, XV, 1893, pp. 75—76, fig. 4).

compromise between the palmette and some such moulding. Borders were
introduced into the illumination of manuscripts at an early period : they occur
in the Vienna manuscript of Dioscorides, and their original use has been conjecturally assigned to the ancient art of Mesopotamia.

The following iconographical points may be noticed in connection with this
ivory.

The representation of the beardless and youthful Christ seated upon the
rainbow, or as here upon the throne, was a favourite subject in the early Middle
Ages. In this aspect Christ is regarded as Emmanuel, the incarnate Logos
removed from the changes of mortality and possessed of eternal youth. To
give effect to this idea, the youthful types of Christ, which early Christian art
derived from Hellenistic sources, were retained long after the bearded or
Nazarene type had come into general use. In the West, this youthful Christ is
frequent to the close of the Romanesque period, while in the East it continued
even later. For in Byzantine art it was usual always so to represent Christ in
scenes which have no direct relation to his earthly career : he is so seen for
example on the famous dalmatic in St Peter's at Rome, which modern criticism
assigns to a later date than the twelfth century. The usual marks of the
Emmanuel type are the open book or roll and the gesture of benediction.

The rainbow or the throne within the glory or mandorla are intended to
suggest the same idea of universal dominion implied by the globe on which
Christ is seated in many early mosaics and even in one of the frescoes of the
catacombs[1]. Christ upon the throne is seen in the sixth century mosaics of
S. Michele in Affricisco, now in the Kaiser Friedrich Museum at Berlin, and
one of the mural paintings at Bawît in Egypt, of about the same date. The
conception is that known as the Majestas Domini, the elements of which are
already to be found in St Jerome's commentaries on Isaiah (ch. vi), Ezekiel
(ch. i and x), and Daniel (ch. vii). In these commentaries there is mention of
the throne, of the rainbow seat, explained as the sign of the covenant between
God and man, as well as of the Evangelists or their symbols.

The glory or mandorla, so common in mediaeval sculpture and painting, is
so called because its pointed oval shape resembles that of an almond ; it is to
the whole body what the nimbus is to the head. It was of quite early occurrence
in Christian art, being found for instance in the nave-mosaics of S. Maria
Maggiore at Rome, which no critics place later than the fourth or early fifth
century, while by some they are assigned to an even earlier date[2].

---

[1] E.g. mosaics of Sta Costanza at Rome, S. Vitale at Ravenna, the lost mosaics of
S. Agatha at Rome. The frescoes are in the Cemetery of S. Priscilla and in the Basilica
of SS. Felix and Adauctus in the Cemetery of Commodilla : the former are assigned
by Wilpert to the 4th, the latter to the 6th century.

[2] J. P. Richter and A. Cameron Taylor, *The Golden Age of Classic Christian Art.*
The mandorla surrounds the figure of the central angel in the scene under the oak at
Mamre. Other early examples are in the mural paintings at Bawît in Egypt, where they
surround Christ as infant and Christ enthroned (J. Clédat, *Mém. de l'Institut français
d'arch. orientale du Caire*, XII, 1904, p's. xc, xci, xcvi) ; the apse mosaic in the church of

The symbols of the Evangelists, almost from the time when they were first used in Christian art, have been usually associated with representations of our Lord in majesty. On the fourth-century ivory in the Trivulzi Collection at Milan (E. Molinier, *Ivoires*, pl. vi), perhaps the earliest instance of their use, only two are present, and the scene depicts the empty tomb of Christ, with the angel and the Holy Women. In the earliest mosaics of Naples and Ravenna all four were grouped about central symbols (the sacred monogram or the Lamb) representing Our Lord. In the frescoes at Bawît in Egypt, none of which are likely to be later than the seventh century, the four visionary beasts surround the figure of our Lord. (J. Clédat, *Mémoires de l'Institut français d'archéologie orientale du Caire*, pls. xc, xci.)

The symbols became far more popular in Western than in Byzantine art. They occur in our own islands in the famous Lindisfarne Gospels of about A.D. 700 (The Durham Book, British Museum, Cotton MS., Nero D. IV) and from this time onward are very frequent in Western painting and sculpture, especially in Romanesque representations of the Majestas Domini. In the East, they do not seem to occur until the late Byzantine period: after the closer contact with the West which followed the fourth crusade, they become more common. Mr Herbert's claim that the symbols are characteristically Western may be regarded as just (*Burlington Magazine*, Vol. XIII, June, 1908).

35. PANEL. An archbishop, beardless and with curly hair, stands facing the spectator, with his left hand holding open a book upon a desk the side of which is carved with double arches in two tiers; his right hand is raised in the gesture of benediction. Behind his head is a scalloped niche, and above this, seen in three-quarter figure, five servers or deacons stand before a second niche of the same character. Before him in a semicircle stand seven canons in the act of singing, with hands extended or raised. At the top and bottom of the panel is a crenelated wall interrupted by pairs of towers with round arched windows. The whole is inclosed within a finely carved border of acanthus leaves.

The archbishop wears an alb; a tunicle (dalmatic) with orfreys ornamented at intervals with raised loop-like ornaments in pairs, one on either side, and with a border of embroidered crosses at the extremity of the sleeves; an embroidered and fringed stole; a

Panagia Kanakaria in the Carpass, Cyprus; a miniature in the gospels of Etchmiadzin (J. Strzygowski, *Byzantinische Denkmäler*, Vol. I), none of which are later than the 7th century.

chasuble cut square at the neck and apparently made to open
down to the breast; and a pallium fringed at the end and fastened
over the breast with a pin. The canons wear albs, rochets, and
hooded copes or almuses; the deacons tunicles with orfreys ornamented in the same manner as that of the archbishop. The
archbishop and canons are all tonsured.

Plate VI. Carolingian, 9th century.

H. 13½ in. B. 5⅜ in. From the Spitzer Collection. Figured : *La Collection
Spitzer*, Paris, 1900, Vol. I, *Ivoires*, pl. v ; E. Molinier, *Ivoires*, pl. xii ; Rohault
de Fleury, *La Messe*, VI, pl. 478. On these panels see Darcel, in *La Collection
Spitzer*, as above, p. 22 ; Molinier, as above, p. 133 ; Westwood, *Fictile Ivories*,
p. 448 ; W. Bode, *Die deutsche Plastik*, Berlin, 1887, p. 9 ; F. C. Ebrard,
Die Stadtbibliothek in Frankfurt am Main, Frankfurt, 1896, pp. 173—174 and
179 ; Rohault de Fleury, *La Messe*, Vol. I, pl. ix, and Vol. VI, p. 150 (drawing
of Frankfort ivory).

The panel is the companion of that which, very probably since the middle of
the fifteenth century, has ornamented the cover of a fourteenth-century manuscript of the Gospels now preserved in the Stadtbibliothek at Frankfort on the
Main, and represents the same archbishop saying mass (J. D. Passavant,
Erhaben gearbeitete Elfenbeintafel aus dem IX *Jahrhundert in der Frankfurter
Stadtbibliothek*, in *Archiv für Frankfurts Geschichte und Kunst*, Vol. I, pp. 132 ff.,
and pl. iv). The book is mentioned in an inventory of the Cathedral Sacristy
dating from A.D. 1450 as a gift of one Hartmann Becker, and Passavant con-
cludes with probability that the binding in its present form is of that period.
From the cathedral it passed into the library of the Bartholomäusstift, and on
the secularisation of that institution in 1803 was transferred to the municipal
library. There is no reason to believe that the McClean panel ever ornamented
the other cover of the book, and the story that it was stolen in 1803 is apocryphal.
The volume shows no sign of its removal, and careful descriptions dating from
the eighteenth century make no mention of it (Hüsgen, *Artistisches Magazin*,
pp. 538 ff. ; Catalogue of the Library of the Bartholomäusstift by Batton, dated
1776). Passavant had plausibly conjectured, though without conclusive evidence,
that the panel at Frankfort may have formed part of the gifts presented by
Lewis the German to the churches in that town. However that may be the two
covers have clearly been separated for a great length of time, perhaps from an
early period in the Middle Ages. From the nature of the two inscriptions
engraved upon the open books it is a fair inference that the ivories were
originally intended to form the covers of a Missal, for in the Cambridge panel
the inscription is the Introit for Advent Sunday which stands at the beginning
of the Missal, while in the Frankfort ivory it has the passage from the Canon
which marks the central and most important part of the service. The words in
the former case, written very incorrectly in a cursive hand, are : *Ad te levavi
animam meam, Deus meus, in te confido, non erubescam: neque irrideant me*

inimici mei: etenim universi qui sustinent te non confundentur (Ps. xxiv. 1—3);
in the latter, *Te igitur, clementissime pater, per Jesum Christum filium tuum
dominum nostrum supplices te rogamur ut accepta (h)abeas et benedicas haec
dona.*

These two panels form a class by themselves, and must be ascribed to an
artist whose work is not represented on any other ivories of the Carolingian
period. Many characteristics indeed they share with these: the strong thick-set
figures, the realism of treatment are found elsewhere. But the peculiar combination of a grandiose if too symmetrical design with the most exact precision
of detail, lends the two panels a peculiar quality of their own. It is difficult to
suppose that work of this kind was executed in the decline of the Carolingian
period: Dr Bode indeed considered it to be actually contemporary with
Charlemagne, pointing to the close resemblance of the architecture with that of
the Carolingian revival. Other authorities are inclined to favour a rather later
date, M. Molinier assigning it to the close of the ninth or the beginning of the
tenth century. But the latter is the extreme limit, and there seems in fact little
reason to cross the boundary of the earlier century. There are unfortunately
few indications which might assist us to assign a more precise date. The
costumes are all ecclesiastical; and as the ivory itself affords one of the best
illustrations of a period when vestments were still undergoing a process of
evolution, the comparative method yields no very certain results.

The documents (*Ordos*) which describe the ceremonial accompanying the
Roman mass do not in their present shape go back further than the close of
the eighth century, and they occasionally differ in points of detail, but it may
be safely assumed that they embody the usages of earlier centuries, and in all
essentials they give us the ceremonial of the sixth or even the fifth century[1].
Before we can form a true idea of its nature, we must eliminate from the
ceremonial of the present day the additions made in the twelfth and thirteenth
centuries, such as the elevation of the Host and Chalice, with the accompanying
lights and torches, censings, bell-ringings and genuflexions. Ritual pomp was
really confined to two moments: the entry of the celebrant into the church and
up to the altar; and to the singing of the gospel. On the occasion of a great
feast when there was a papal or episcopal mass, the procession of the celebrant
and his ministers to the altar consisted of seven acolytes bearing torches, seven
deacons, and seven sub-deacons, all wearing from the Pope or bishop down to
the acolytes, the planeta or chasuble. The choir of singers was already
stationed in the presbyterium ranged in two groups, one on either side of the
sanctuary in front of the altar. The presence of the uneven number of seven
canons upon the ivory may thus be intentional. The archbishop wears the
ample chasuble of the Carolingian period (Rohault de Fleury, *La Messe*,
Vol. VII, pp. 125 ff. and pl. dlxvii), which, as worn by the higher ecclesiastics,
was often of silk enriched with gold and silver thread. Good examples are to

[1] For the statements in this and the following paragraphs, see a paper by Mr
Edmund Bishop read before the Historical Research Society, May 8, 1899.

be seen in the miniatures of the Sacramentary of Drogo formerly at Metz and now in the Bibliothèque Nationale at Paris, where for the first time we notice the kind of hood or capuchon at the back of the neck, much as it appears on the chasubles of the canons upon our ivory (F. X. Kraus, *Kunst und Alterthum in Lothringen*, III, 1889, pls. xiv and xv, and p. 577). It has already been stated in the remarks upon the *Ordos* that the chasuble in the ninth century was by no means the exclusively liturgical vestment which it has since become, and that it was worn by all who took part in the procession at a papal or episcopal mass. In the bible of Charles the Bold, the canons offering the book to the Emperor wear chasubles of bright colours patterned and bordered with gold, and showing the hood at the back.

The pallium, as here shown, is transitional between that of the earlier centuries, which was thrown over the shoulders without attachment, and the various later forms which were permanently made to form a collar with pendants behind and in front. In the present case a pin is used to hold it in position over the breast, perhaps the first example of this attachment known in mediaeval art, for though Rohault de Fleury conjectures that the pallium of the archbishop on the paliotto of S. Ambrogio at Milan (A.D. 835) may have had a pin, it is not to be clearly distinguished. Pallia would appear to have been already sewn as early as the ninth century if we may judge from a Metz MS. of that date in the Bibliothèque Nationale (MS. Lat. 1141), but this method of fixture does not seem to have been general until considerably later, and pins were used as late as the thirteenth century (Rohault de Fleury, *La Messe*, Vol. VIII, Chapter on the pallium).

Good examples of the pallium and chasuble as worn rather later at the close of the tenth century are to be seen in the MSS. connected with Archbishop Egbert of Trèves (A.D. 977—993). See F. X. Kraus, *Die Miniaturen des Codex Egberti*, pl. ii, and Sauerland and Haseloff, *Der Psalter Erzbischof Egberts von Trier*, pl. ii.

It may be observed that the conventional representation of a town by means of a polygonal walled enclosure with towers at intervals, so common with Carolingian and succeeding periods, is an inheritance from earlier times. Places referred to in the *Notitia Dignitatum* are indicated in this manner, and something of the same kind is to be seen in the Vatican MS. of Cosmas Indicopleustes (Cod. Graec. 699).

It is impossible to say where this panel and its companion at Frankfort were made. They do not fall into any of the classes into which Carolingian ivories have been more or less conjecturally divided: and they bear no intrinsic evidence pointing to their place of origin.

36. CASKET of wood, covered with ivory plaques fixed with bone pegs.

The casket is rectangular, the lid approaching the form of a truncated pyramid: each of the sides is ornamented with two sunk panels bordered with narrow plaques carved with formal rosettes. All these panels are carved with animals or monsters, and those of the front and back have on either side strips of intarsia in green, white and black.

On the front are a lion and another quadruped; on the back, the same quadruped and a gryphon; on the left end a gryphon and a lion; on the right end two gryphons: each animal is near a tree. On the oblong panel on the lid, which is bordered by intarsia work, are a gryphon and a quadruped divided by a sacred tree: on the sides and rims are vine and other scroll designs.

Plate VII. Byzantine, 12th century.

L. 9¾ in. B. 7⅝ in. From the Spitzer Collection. *La Collection Spitzer,* I, p. 30. H. Graeven, *Jahrbuch der kunsthistorischen Sammlungen des allerhöchsten Kaiserhauses,* Vol. XX, Vienna, 1899, no. 43, p. 27.

Another casket from the same collection with a flat sliding lid, now in the Brussels Museum, has animals of similar character (Destrée, *Musées Royaux des arts décoratifs et industriels, Catalogue des Ivoires,* 1902, no. 4, p. 17). A third is in the Treasury of the Cathedral of Würzburg (J. von Hefner Alteneck, *Trachten, Kunstwerke und Geräthschaften,* Vol. I, pl. i, Frankfort, 1879). A fourth is in the collection of Henry Oppenheimer, Esq., of London.

This casket, by the character of the borders with rosettes, is allied to the large group of Byzantine caskets with mythological and classical subjects, of which one of the finest and earliest examples is that formerly in the Cathedral of Veroli, and now in the Victoria and Albert Museum at South Kensington (see H. Graeven, *Jahrbuch der kunsthistorischen Sammlungen des allerhöchsten Kaiserhauses,* Vienna, 1899, pp. 5 ff., and *L'Arte,* Vol. II, 1899; A. Venturi, *Le gallerie nazionali italiane,* III, 1897, pp. 261 ff., *L'Arte,* I, 1898, and *Storia dell' arte italiana,* I, pp. 512 ff.; R. von Schneider, *Serta Harteliana,* Vienna, 1896). The Veroli casket probably dates from the ninth century; but from the degeneration in the style of other examples, it is probable that work of this kind continued to be made for some two hundred years. The caskets with mythological subjects are supposed to have first appeared when the iconoclastic persecution compelled the ivory carvers to seek other than religious models; antique silver plate and early miniatures provided the inspiration for the designs. Perhaps at the time when the iconoclastic tradition was a thing of the past and religious subjects were once more prescribed, the caskets with similar rosette borders but with figures of saints &c. and scriptural scenes (the story of Adam and Eve) were manufactured (Graeven, *L'Arte,* 1899; Venturi, *Storia* &c., II, pp. 606—608). It is interesting to note that the small group representing the expulsion from Eden on the bronze door of the Cathedral at Pisa is so very like the representation of the same scene on an ivory panel from a Byzantine casket in the Museo Oliveriano at Pesaro, that Bonannus must have derived his inspiration from an ivory carving of this character. The caskets which, like the present example, have monsters and animals of oriental types in place of human figures, would also appear to be of about the twelfth century. They are rare and were imitated by almost contemporary examples made and preserved in Italy (Museo Civico, Pisa, H. Graeven, *Elfenbeinwerke in photographischer Nachbildung*, Series II, nos. 52—53; Venturi, *Storia dell' arte italiana*, II, p. 607; the Museo Civico at Ravenna, Graeven, as above, no. 54; and the Cathedral of Ivrea, Venturi, as above, pp. 613—615). The intarsia upon the present casket must be regarded as a subsequent addition. Work of this kind made of coloured bone and horn was commonly described as *alla certosina* because practised so largely by the Carthusians of Lombardy and Venetia. It is of oriental origin, and was introduced into Italy about the fourteenth century; it was frequently employed to enrich the carved bone caskets made in the workshops of the Embriachi at Venice (see J. von Schlosser, in *Jahrbuch der kunsthistorischen Sammlungen* &c., Vienna, Vol. XX, 1899, p. 238). The somewhat similar work produced in modern Bombay was introduced into India from Persia rather more than a century ago.

37. PANEL, from the cover of McClean MS. no. 30, a *Lectionarium* of the second half of the tenth century from Reichenau, S. Germany. A half-figure of Our Lord, facing, in tunic and pallium. He holds the Book of the Gospels in his left hand, and with the fingers of his right makes the gesture of benediction. Behind Our Lord's head are seen the three upper limbs of the cross, the surfaces chequered in the same way as the cover of the Gospels in his hand. Above and below, an acanthus border.

Plate VIII. Byzantine, 11—12th century.
H. 5⅝ in. B. 3⅞ in.
The figure resembles that upon a relief in the Louvre (Molinier, *Catalogue des ivoires*, no. 14), a circumstance which has raised some doubt as to the authenticity of the present panel. The unusual large cross behind the head lends some colour to the supposition; but at present there does not appear to be sufficient evidence to condemn the work. Dr Adolf Merton has called attention to a half-figure of the Virgin and Child on the cover of a tenth-century Evangelistary in the Stadtbibliothek at Leipsic, which is also from Reichenau, and is a companion-volume to McClean MS. 30. This panel is in a similar style, the drapery being treated in the same summary and mechanical manner.

38. SUNK PANEL, with plain narrow borders: the Crucifixion beneath a pierced canopy supported on two slender columns, above which are busts of angels. Our Lord wears a broad loincloth, and

his feet rest upon a *suppedaneum*. To right and left stand the
Virgin and St John, the latter holding the book of his Gospel.
Above are the sun and moon. The cross is fixed by three wedges,
below which is seen the skull of Adam.

Along the top of the panel is pegged a narrow strip of ivory
carved with foliations and rosettes.

Plate VIII. Byzantine, 11*th—*12*th century.*
H. 4$\frac{11}{16}$ in. Formerly in the Spitzer Collection.
The lower border is pierced with several holes and there is a hole in each
side-border towards the bottom. In the top of the pierced canopy is fixed
a gilded stud or nail.
The Crucifixion is treated in the most usual Byzantine manner; the group
is rigidly symmetrical, and there is a tranquillity about the whole scene which
excludes the idea of dramatic action.
The wedges driven in at the base to fix the cross are a constant Byzantine
feature, as is the skull of Adam, which is frequently found in Western mediaeval
art (cf. no. 55). An ancient legend ran that the remains of the first man were
interred upon the very spot where the cross was erected, and the belief was
adopted by the encyclopaedic writers like Honorius of Autun whose works
exercised a direct influence upon representative art. "In loco Calvariae sepultus
[Adam] aliquamdiu requievit" (Honorius, *De imagine Mundi,* III, in Migne,
Patr. Lat. 172).

39. DIPTYCH. Each leaf has two zones divided by a band of
rosettes, with a similar band of rosettes along the top. All the
subjects are beneath architectural canopies.

Left leaf. Above are the Annunciation and the Salutation;
below, the Virgin crowned, standing with the Child flanked by two
angels holding candlesticks. The Virgin holds a flower and the
Child a fruit.

Right leaf. Above, the Last Judgment. Below, the Crucifixion
between the Virgin and St John. Our Lord is enthroned between
two angels holding the Instruments of the Passion, and the
kneeling figures of the Virgin and St John: in a trefoiled compartment beneath the dead are seen issuing from their tombs.

Plate IX. French, First half of the 14*th century.*
H. 7 in. B. 6$\frac{1}{2}$ in.
The hinges are modern; the tapers from the candlesticks borne by the
angels are broken off.
The Last Judgment in this abbreviated form is found on other ivories of the

period, e.g. the diptych in the Louvre (R. Koechlin in A. Michel's *Histoire de l'art*, p. 485, fig. 320).

The complete version of this scene as conceived by the artists of the Gothic period includes the weighing of the souls, the separation of the righteous from the lost, &c. as represented in the sculptures of Laon, Chartres, Paris, Amiens, and Bourges. The Gothic tradition, based upon St Matthew as well as Revelation, with additions such as the introduction of the Virgin and St John as intercessors, was embodied in the *Elucidarium* of Vincent de Beauvais (ch. xi).

A minor point of interest is that the dead are all represented as in the prime of life, it being held that all will rise of the same age as that of Our Lord at his crucifixion, namely thirty years.

For the whole subject, see E. Male, *L'art religieux du* XIIIe *siècle en France*, pp. 465 ff.; for the Last Judgment in English Gothic sculpture, W. R. Lethaby, *Archaeologia*, Vol. LX, pp. 379 ff.

40. RIGHT LEAF OF A DIPTYCH, subjects in two zones under architectural canopies.

Below. The Nativity and Annunciation to the shepherds.

Above. The Coronation of the Virgin.

Plate X. French, First half of the 14th century.

H. 6⅛″. B. 3¾″. From the Bateman Collection (Catalogue, Sotheby's, April, 1893, no. 35).

The holes for hinges are on the left. There is a hole at the top of the panel in the middle.

The Coronation of the Virgin is a subject unknown to Early Christian and Byzantine art, and only becoming common in the West with the thirteenth century. It is not directly suggested by any passage either of Scripture or legend but indications from various sources combined to stimulate the artists' imagination until the typical rendering was evolved. Thus in the *Golden Legend* Christ is made to say, "Come from Lebanon and receive the Crown": and the Virgin comes and seats herself by the side of her son: while the verse of the Psalm, *astitit regina a dextris ejus in vestitu deaurato*, may have served to complete the ideal picture (see E. Male, *L'art religieux du* XIIIe *siècle*, p. 328).

41. LEFT LEAF OF A DIPTYCH, subjects in two zones under architectural canopies.

Above. The Crucifixion between the Virgin and St John; the Virgin is supported by two women. Behind St John stand two Jews in pointed caps.

Below. The Murder of Becket.

To *r.* is the altar, behind which stands a priest holding out a cross. Before it kneels Becket attacked from behind by the three knights.

Plate X. French, First half of the 14th century.

H. 4$\frac{7}{16}$ in. From the Magniac Collection (Sale Catalogue, Christie's, 1892, no. 256).

The type of the Crucifixion is one commonly found in French ivories. The subject of the lower zone would not, in any case, justify the assumption that this ivory is English, as the martyrdom of Becket is of frequent occurrence upon French works of art, notably on the enamelled reliquaries of Limoges. The subject is rare upon ivory carvings, but need not arouse suspicion, as it appears on a diptych-leaf figured in the *Gentleman's Magazine* for 1786 (Vol. LVI, p. 925, and plate for November). It is found, again below the Crucifixion, on another leaf of a diptych of the fourteenth century, no. 486 of the Homberg Collection, Sale Catalogue, Paris, 1908.

42. TRIPTYCH. The centre and leaves have all two zones, the scenes in each case being surmounted by crocketed canopies. The sequence of subjects begins at the bottom left-hand corner with the interview of Judas and the Jews; the next scenes, the Betrayal and death of Judas, occupy the bottom of the central panel; on the bottom of the right leaf is the Flagellation. Passing to the upper compartment of the left leaf, we find Our Lord bearing his cross on the road to Calvary; on the central panel, the Crucifixion between the Virgin and St John, and the Descent from the Cross; and in the upper compartment of the right leaf the Entombment.

Plate X. French, middle of the 14th century.

H. 5$\frac{7}{8}$ in. Total breadth 8$\frac{7}{8}$ in.

In the Death of Judas, one leg is broken off. In the Flagellation, the column is broken. The hands of several figures are also damaged. There are traces of red pigment and gilding upon the architecture. The subjects of fourteenth-century ivories are often arranged as here so as to be read from the bottom, in the same way as in stained-glass windows.

43. GROUP: the Virgin and Child seated on a throne with high back on the top of which stand small figures of angels playing musical instruments. To the left stands St Elizabeth holding a basket and a bunch of roses; to the right, St Catherine with wheel and sword.

Plate XI. Spanish, 16th century.

H. 8$\frac{7}{8}$ in.

ENAMELS.

44. BRONZE TWO-HANDLED VASE, turned on the lathe, decorated with champlevé enamel in seven horizontal bands.

1 (top).   Vertical sprigs side by side on a red ground.

2.   Maeander on a green? ground.

3.   A conventional garland on red.

4.   A vine scroll with birds, on orange.

5.   A lozenge chequer of red, green and orange in horizontal bands.

6.   As no. 3, but the ground alternately red and green.   On the outer side of the handles is a herring-bone pattern; on the base, concentric turned circles.

Plate XII.   Provincial Roman, 3rd century.

H. 4¼ in.   From the Forman Collection (Catalogue, Sotheby's, June, 1899, no. 168).

The colours have largely perished, and some are not easy to determine with certainty.

For enamels of the class represented by this vase and the following numbers see Introduction, p. 39.

45. BRONZE PRICKET CANDLESTICK, decorated with champlevé enamel.   Round the pan are squares and vandykes alternately blue and white; round the upper part of the base a laurel wreath on a green (?) ground ; on the lower part a vandyked design coloured blue and white, the blue triangles each having an orange-red spot.   On the bottom edge, a row of rectangles once enamelled·

Plate XII.   Provincial Roman, 3rd century.

H. 3¾ in.   From the Magniac Collection (Catalogue, Christie's, July, 1892, no. 661).

Perhaps made on the Meuse.

46. BRONZE INKPOT (?), with champlevé enamel.   It is shaped like an egg-cup, with a flat mouth partly closed, and a small baluster stopper clipping by means of a slot.

Round the sides are three zones, two with gadroons alternately red, blue and green (?), the third with radiating rays on similar grounds. Inside the top, and on the top of the stopper, are bands of red enamel. The stopper is pierced lengthwise.

Plate XII. Provincial Roman, 3rd century.
H. 3¼ in. From the Forman Collection, no. 169.
The use of this object is conjectural.

47—51. FIVE FRAGMENTS. On one, the head and shoulders of a beardless inscribed figure in a mandorla are reserved in the metal on a background of lapis blue on which are reserved scrolls : similar scrolls are in the spandrels. Another, belonging to the same plaque, has the lower part of a figure seated on the rainbow within a mandorla (Our Lord).

The third and fourth make the complete figure of a sainted archbishop with a crozier, beneath a round arch ; the last, a smaller and almost triangular fragment, has part of a wing.

Plate XXI. French, Limoges, 12th century.
Dimensions from 4¾ in. to 2¾ in. Formerly in the Magniac Collection (no. 250 B).
The edges of these fragments have been bevelled and morticed, and in one a hole has been made for a lock. A great deal of the enamel is lost. The colours used are lapis blue, turquoise, green, yellow, red, white, and a pink for faces and hands. The figures are in some cases reserved on an enamelled ground, in others enamelled on a ground punched with quatrefoils, stars and circles, as in the case of the book-cover no. 55, and of a pax in the Musée de Cluny at Paris (E. Rupin, *L'œuvre de Limoges*, p. 571 ; Rohault de Fleury, *La Messe*, VI, pl. 496, and Du Sommerard, *Les arts au Moyen Âge*, Album, 2nd series, pl. xxxix).

52. END OF A RELIQUARY, champlevé enamel on copper.
On a background of lapis blue enamel relieved by a scroll design reserved in the metal, the stems terminating in flowers of coloured enamel, two bearded saints, also reserved in the metal, are seated with their feet resting upon footstools of turquoise blue. They are crowned and wear long garments ; the nimbus of each is enamelled with various shades of green, blue and white. Below is a broad reserved band with an inscription filled with blue enamel : EXVLTABVNT : DÑO : OSSA : HVMILIATA (Psalm li. 8). Below this is a wavy band of dark and light blue enamel variegated with spots of red. At the bottom are two sarcophagi the fronts of which are ornamented with strigils in green, blue and red : they are without

lids, and within them are seen skulls and bones in white enamel. Between them is a floral scroll. All the metal is gilt; and the details of the figures engraved.

Plate XIV. Limoges, 13th century.

H. 9½ in. B. 7 in. Formerly in the Debruge Dumenil and Hastings Collections. J. Labarte, *Description des objets d'art qui composent la collection Debruge Dumenil*, Paris, 1847, no. 681, p. 581.

The companion panel, which in 1847 was in private hands at Lyon, is illustrated and described in Cahier and Martin's *Mélanges d'archéologie Chrétienne*, Vol. I, pl. 44 and p. 247. It was sold at the sale of the collection of M. Homberg in May, 1908. It has two similar saints seated in the same manner above two open sarcophagi, but the strigils in this case are yellow, and the inscription is:

CVSTODIT DNS OMNIA OSSA SⱢOR (Custodit Dominus omnia ossa Sanctorum, Psalm l. 10).

The representation of coffins with strigils upon the sides is probably due to the imitation of classical sarcophagi. It occurs again upon the end of a Limoges enamelled reliquary in the Carrand Collection in the Bargello at Florence (*Les Arts*, July, 1904, p. 10).

53. QUATREFOIL PLAQUE, enamelled copper. On a metal ground punched with circles and quatrefoils is a figure of an angel holding a cross in his right hand. He wears a dark blue mantle bordered with paler blue and white; his wings are enamelled with three shades of blue, red and white; his hair and eyes are dark blue; his nimbus turquoise with yellow rim. Round the plaque runs an enamelled wavy border with bands of red, dark blue, white, and turquoise.

Limoges, 13th century.

D. 3⅜ in. Formerly in the Magniac Collection (Sale Catalogue, Christie's, 1892, no. 665).

54. CRUCIFIX, enamelled copper upon oak, with an applied bronze figure of Christ. The ground of the enamel is of lapis blue dotted with small lozenges and circles of green and yellow, and red and white, with red centres. Round the edges runs a border of white shading into pale and dark blue, and the ends of the arms terminate in quadruple wavy bands in red, dark blue, pale blue and white. The central cross to which the figure is applied is dark green shading off to pale green and yellow: the *suppedaneum* on which the feet rest is dark blue, and has on it white circles with red centres. The nimbus is of concentric circles of red, dark blue, pale blue and white, and the cross contained in it is red and yellow. The lower extremity is occupied by imbrications of various colours representing the rocks of Golgotha. At the top of the upper limb, reserved in the metal, is the hand of the Almighty, and below this, on two transverse reserved bands, the inscription IH̅S X̅P̅S; on the lower limb a beardless figure is represented rising from a tomb, the whole also reserved in the metal. To the back of this limb is nailed a plaque of gilt copper ornamented with a punched scroll design enclosing two circular spaces to which medallions were probably applied. The Christ is not in the round, but a hollow half-figure without back: it is in the usual style, crowned, and with inlaid black enamel eyes, the feet pierced with two separate nails, and the muscles of the arms conventionally represented by punched lines. Like all the other metal-work upon the cross, it was formerly gilded.

Limoges, 13th century.

H. 13⅜ in. B. 7⅛ in.

The enamel had been damaged in several places: between the Dextera Domini and the nimbus, and at the extremities of the top, bottom and left limbs. In all these places it has been restored with a coloured and varnished composition.

The figure issuing from the tomb below the cross represents Adam, and occurs both in Carolingian and Byzantine art (see E. Molinier, *Gazette des Beaux-Arts*, 1898, p. 483).

55. PANEL FROM A BOOK-COVER; THE CRUCIFIXION between the Virgin and St John. The figure of Our Lord is in relief, the two others reserved in the metal. His feet rest upon a *suppedaneum*, below which is the skull of Adam. On the upper limb of the cross are a titulus with IH̅S X̅P̅S and the Dextera Domini; and on either side of it the bust of an angel holding a book. The cross, which is green, rises from an imbricated hill, and across the whole panel run two bands of turquoise enamel. The ground is of lapis blue, enriched with rosettes of various colours.

Plate XV. French (Limoges), 13th century.

H. 9½ in.

For the skull of Adam cf. the enamelled book-covers formerly in the Spitzer Collection (*La Collection Spitzer*, Vol. I, *Orfèvrerie religieuse*, no. 48, p. 113, and no. 59, p. 116). Examples of its occurrence are numerous in Western as well as in Byzantine art. For the tradition that the first man was buried upon Golgotha, see no. 38 above.

The imbricated mount below the cross is frequent; cf. a panel in the Collection of M. O. Homberg, which also has the transverse bands of turquoise (*Les Arts*, December, 1904, p. 39). It is also seen on the earlier diptych known as the diptych of Rambona in the Vatican Library (R. Kanzler, *Gli avori* &c., pl. v, and Venturi, *Storia dell' arte italiana*, II, p. 174).

56. ORNAMENTS OF A BOOK-COVER. The manuscript, which contains the Hours of the Virgin bound in green velvet, has rivetted to both covers champlevé enamels consisting in each case of a central plaque and four narrow bands forming a border.

On the upper cover the plaque, which is oval and of the shape of a mandorla, has reserved in the metal a beardless saint standing to the right, grasping his mantle in his left hand and holding his right over his breast. He wears beneath his mantle a tunic with a broad hatched collar, and has an enamelled nimbus with concentric bands of red, green and yellow. The background is of lapis blue crossed by two horizontal bands of turquoise and enriched with six discs each of three colours, red, green and yellow, or red, blue and white. The narrow plaque at the top of the border is horizontally divided by a band of zigzag in red: the three triangular spaces below this are filled by busts of angels reserved in the metal upon a lapis ground; the spaces above, by a diaper of small reserved crosses on the same ground. The plaque at the bottom is similarly ornamented, except that the zigzag band is white, and the lower triangular spaces are filled by a bird, a quadruped and a wyvern. The side plaques, which resemble each other, have the same diaper of reserved crosses, on which is a row of reserved lozenges with red edges, each containing an enamelled quatrefoil in red, blue and green.

The lower cover has in the middle a similar saint to right, but the lapis blue background is enriched with small reserved lozenges instead of enamelled discs. The plaque forming the border at the top is similar to that on the upper cover, but has only two angels, beyond which at either end are smaller triangles with foliate design: the bottom border has three wyverns and part of a foliation; the sides are like those of the upper cover.

Plate XVI. 13th century.

H. 7⅛ in. B. 4⅛⅛ in.

The enamel in the quatrefoils and bands of zigzag is considerably damaged. The plaques forming the borders have been cut from longer strips.

The style of the central plaques has suggested doubts as to their authenticity. Other narrow borders of a similar kind are to be seen in the Galerie d'Apollon in the Louvre: cf. also Du Sommerard, *Les Arts au Moyen Âge*, Album, Series II, pl. xxxviii, and the Casket, no. 58 below. The arrangement of reserved animals, &c. in a band of lozenges occurs on the narrow enamelled strips which ornament the reliquaries made on the Rhine in the second half of the twelfth century. See Von Falke, *Deutsche Schmelzarbeiten* &c., coloured plates xxi—xxiii, and cf. J. J. Marquet de Vasselot, *La Collection Martin Le Roy*, I, pls. x and xi.

57. SUNK OAK PANEL, covered with gilt copper plaques, and having in the middle the Crucifixion between the Virgin and St John, in champlevé enamel. On a background of gilt copper punched with quatrefoils and rosettes is an enamelled cross of lapis blue semé with discs composed of various colours in concentric bands: to this is applied a figure of Our Lord resembling that of no. 2, but with a dark blue loincloth, the feet resting upon a *suppedaneum* of turquoise blue. On the upper limb of the cross is a band reserved in the metal, with the letters IHS XPS filled with turquoise blue enamel. On either side of the cross are applied figures of the Virgin and St John, the former wearing a dark blue mantle over a paler blue tunic, and having her hands crossed over the breast; the latter in a mantle of similar colour over a green tunic, holding in his left hand the book of his Gospel enamelled in red and white, and raising his right hand before his breast. Both figures stand upon footstools of turquoise blue: the eyes are in each case formed by vitreous black beads. Above the arms of the cross are two applied busts of angels, each raising the right hand and holding a book in the left. Their mantles are enamelled in red, white and lapis blue, their tunics with green and yellow, their wings with yellow, lapis and turquoise. The background is enriched by rows of cabochon glass pastes of red, blue, and dark and light green in raised settings.

The raised border is covered with gilt metal punched as before with quatrefoils and stars over which are applied at the four corners angular plaques having scrolls reserved in the metal on a lapis blue ground, and in the angle, medallions of turquoise blue containing reserved metal stars. Between these corner plates are four small rectangular plaques with large reserved stars on turquoise blue grounds, and cabochon pastes in square raised settings.

Limoges, 13th century.
H. 12⅜ in. B. 7¼ in.

The right-hand angel, the angular plaques at the right-hand top and left-hand bottom corners and the small plaques in the middle of the border at top and bottom are brighter in colour than the other enamels which suggests the possibility that they are restorations.

Formerly in the Sneyd Collection at Keele Hall. On the back are labels showing that it was exhibited at the Art Treasures Exhibition at Manchester in 1857, and in the National Exhibition of Works of Art at Leeds in 1868. The style is that of certain Limoges reliquaries of the thirteenth century covered in the same way with engraved copper plaques ornamented with cabochon pastes and applied figures fixed by rivets. A reliquary formerly in the Spitzer Collection had the Crucifixion similarly represented (*La Collection Spitzer*, Paris, 1900, Vol. I, *Orfèvrerie religieuse*, pl. x, no. 26). A panel in the same style with the same subject is upon a book-cover in the treasury of the Cathedral of Lyon (L. Bégule, *Monographie de la cathédrale de Lyon*, plate opposite p. 206). Another forms one side of a textus cover figured by Du Sommerard, *Les Arts au Moyen Âge*, Album, Series III, pl. xxii. A casket in the Museum at Copenhagen may also be compared (Stephens, *Runic Monuments*, I, p. 476 c).

58. CASKET. The sides are overlaid with thin plates of silver with embossed figures of angels holding books, under round arches; the spandrels, which are gilt, are ornamented with embossed vine-scrolls.

The lid is of a truncated pyramidal form. Along the top is a strip of silver embossed with palmettes: the rest is covered with champlevé enamel. On the sides is a series of turquoise blue lozenges enclosing reserved quatrefoils on a ground of lapis blue, the whole within a border of reserved leaves on a red ground. On one end is an expanded flower in various colours (green, yellow, white, turquoise blue and lilac purple); on the other, a symmetrical design of floral scrolls in lapis, turquoise, pale blue, yellow, white and red on a ground of maroon.

Plate XVII. Rhenish, 12th century.
L. 4¾ in. H. 2½ in. From the Magniac Collection (Catalogue, Christie's, 1902, no. 496).

The date of this casket is probably not far from the year 1200. The details of its ornament both in enamel and in the embossed metal are of types which begin to be widely used in the twelfth century. Thus the large leaf at one end of the lid is a development of an earlier form, beginning, in illuminated MSS., towards A.D. 1140 and continuing popular in all branches of art down to the first quarter of the thirteenth century. In the later part of the period it is frequently used to fill the volutes of the enamelled croziers of Limoges. The peculiar form of palmette embossed upon the top of the lid is a variant of the "enclosed palmette" very popular in Romanesque art, and occurring for example on the great Kronleuchter at Hildesheim, as well as on the crestings of the large reliquaries made on the Rhine and the Meuse in the twelfth century.

The enamels upon the sides somewhat resemble those upon the book-covers (no. 56) and would appear to be later than those of the lid : the casket as it stands is thus a composite made up of elements of different dates, the earliest parts being of the twelfth century. A purple maroon colour somewhat resembling that on the lid of this casket is also found on these Rhenish enamels, e.g. on the Annoschrein at Siegburg, ascribed to Cologne, A.D. 1183 (Falke, pll. xiv, xv).

59. CIBORIUM, of gilt copper with enamel.

From a foot of six semicircular lobes separated by small redans, rises a cylindrical stem with hexagonal knop. The cup and its cover are both hemispherical, and fastened by a hinge and hasp : an undecorated circular space on the top of the lid marks the place where a vertical stem, surmounted by a cross, was formerly fixed.

On the cover are four arches in the Gothic style reserved in the metal within which, on a lapis blue ground semé of reserved stars, are four scenes from the Passion, also reserved. These are Christ mocked, the Flagellation, the Road to Calvary, and the Crucifixion. The nimbuses in these scenes are enamelled with turquoise blue : the spandrels between the arches are red, with reserved trefoils. On the cup are six circular medallions with grounds alternately of red and turquoise, on which are reserved standing figures of angels : the spandrels have scrolls reserved on a dark blue ground. On the foot are six similar medallions with angels, the upper spandrels having trefoils, the lower fleurs-de-lys, all reserved in the metal.

Plate XVIII. Limoges, 14th century.

H. 9 in. Formerly in the Magniac Collection (Sale Catalogue, Christie's, 1892, no. 500).

This ciborium is of the usual form made at Limoges in the fourteenth century. A similar example was in the Spitzer Collection (*La Collection Spitzer*, Vol. I, *Orfèvrerie religieuse*, no. 58, p. 116).

60. ENAMELLED BRASS CANDLESTICK. The base is oval, the stem broad and flat, the socket in the form of the calyx of a flower. The design is of white flowers on a blue ground, and is executed by the champlevé process.

Plate XIX. English, 17*th century.*
H. 9 in. From the Magniac Collection.
See Introduction, p. 54.
Examples of similar candlesticks in the British and Victoria and Albert Museums are reproduced by Mr J. Starkie Gardner in *Some Minor Arts,* 1894, p. 79. The Victoria and Albert Museum, and the Free Public Museums, Liverpool, also possess fire-dogs enamelled in the same manner.

61. CHALICE of silver and copper-gilt. The foot has twelve lobes alternately semicircular and pointed. To the semicircular lobes correspond six applied six-foil silver plaques with translucent enamels on sunk relief; to the pointed lobes correspond smaller triangular plaques: between the enamels are floral designs in relief. The subjects of the larger plaques are the Crucifixion, with the Instruments of the Passion, on either side of which are the Virgin and St John, and, on the opposite side, a bishop with mitre and crozier between a male and a female saint: the smaller plaques are enamelled with cherubs and trefoil designs. The hexagonal stem, divided into two parts by a knop, rises from a series of mouldings, between the lower of which is a plain band with the inscription in Lombardic letters: ANDREA PETRUCI DE SENIS ME FECI[T]. Both above and below the knop each face of the stem is engraved with a male bust without the nimbus; the knop is ornamented with leaves in relief between which are applied six six-foil silver plaques with translucent enamel representing two male and four female saints.

The cup is contained within a false-cup of silver resembling a calyx, on which are six medallions containing Our Lord, St Peter, St Paul, St John, St Bartholomew, St Barnabas (?).

Plate XX. Sienese, late 14*th century.*
H. 7½ in. D. of cup 3⅝ in. Magniac Collection (Sale Catalogue, Christie's, 1892, no. 798).
This chalice is of the type commonly made in the North of Italy in the late fourteenth century, especially at Siena (see Introduction, p. 56). It may

be compared with three in the Spitzer Collection (*La Collection Spitzer*, Vol. I, *L'orfèvrerie religieuse*, nos. 78, 80, 81).

For Sienese goldsmiths see G. Milanesi, *Documenti per la storia dell' arte Sienese*, Siena 1854—1856.

62. SILVER FRAME OF A TRIPTYCH, parcel gilt and enamelled, the metal taking the form of traceried windows with trefoil arches surmounted by quatrefoil and trefoil openings. In the two trefoil openings are plaques of translucent enamel, that on the left representing a beardless saint holding a palm and book (?), that on the right a bearded saint holding a book and raising his right hand in the gesture of benediction. The chief colours are green, purple and blue, the latter used for the backgrounds.

The enamels French, 14th century.
H. 7⅜ in. From the Magniac Collection (no. 337).
The tracery is to a great extent modern, and the wooden back, painted with a diaper, is also modern.

PAINTED ENAMELS.

63. CIRCULAR PLAQUE: THE ADORATION OF THE MAGI. To the left the Virgin is seated on a carved wooden seat without back, holding out the Child to the first of the three kings, who kneels to present a casket with the two other kings behind him. In the background behind the Virgin is a building with a gable end; to the right is the open country; in the blue sky is seen the star. The Virgin has a purple nimbus, and wears a blue tunic with purple mantle ornamented down the front with discs of foil. The kneeling king, whose hair and beard are yellow, wears a turquoise blue tunic and purple mantle, with a broad white collar. Of the standing kings, the first has a green tunic and purple mantle, and wears a crown enriched with foils; the other, a beardless youth with long hair, wears blue nether garments and a brown sleeveless jerkin, below which is a green tunic.

Plate XXIII. French, Limoges, late 15th century.
D. 2·5 in. From the Magniac Collection (no. 516).
The plaque is in the style of Nardon Penicaud and may be attributed to an enameller of his school. Two similar circular plaques, one with the Ecce Homo, the other with a Pietà, are in the Ashmolean Museum at Oxford.

64. PANEL, THE ADORATION OF THE MAGI; in grisaille. On the left the Virgin is seated with the Child; behind her stands Joseph, while the most aged of the three Magi, with a long white beard, kneels before her, touching the Child's foot with his right hand. The two other kings stand behind him holding cups; the youngest, in the foreground, wears high boots with slashed tops, and spurs. On the right, armed retainers hold the horses; one of them carries a banner. Background of architecture, with a central pier, to right and left of which are distant views of hills with castles; in the sky is seen the Star, from which issue brilliant rays. In the foreground, a broken column.

> *Plate XXI. French, Limoges, 16th century.*
> L. 6 in.

This rich and animated composition, apparently reproducing a work by a German master, is found on two almost identical plaques, both now in Paris. One, formerly in the Spitzer Collection, is in the Collection Dutuit (*La Collection Dutuit, Cent Planches*, 1908, pl. 43 with note by M. J. J. Marquet de Vasselot); the other, formerly at Hamilton Palace, belongs to Baron Edouard de Rothschild (*Catalogue of the Collection...of the Duke of Hamilton*, Christie's, 1882, p. 119, no. 973, and *The Hamilton Palace Collection*, illustrated, 1882, p. 127). The latter example has on the broken column in the foreground the letters MP, the initials of an enameller at present unidentified.

The occurrence of the same composition upon three plaques need not militate against their genuineness, for many subjects were repeated by the enamellers of Limoges, especially those derived from popular engravings. Hitherto it has been impossible to assign the original of this Adoration to any known artist.

65. PANEL IN GRISAILLE: THE LAST SUPPER. In a polygonal chamber with oval windows Our Lord is seated at a round table with the twelve apostles. Above, is a hanging lamp with two flames. On the sides of the benches are classical figures and floral scrolls. On a cornice of the chamber, to the right, is the signature P.R. 1542.

> *Plate XXII. French, Limoges, 16th century.*
> L. 5⅞ in. B. 4¹³⁄₁₆ in. From the Magniac Collection (no. 230).
> By Pierre Reymond.

66. HEXAGONAL SALT, painted in grisaille with subjects illustrating the triumph and endurance of Love, each accompanied by an inscription.

In the circular depression at the top is a bust of Paris wearing a feathered hat: IE SVIS PARIS. Border of cornucopia.

In the corresponding depression at the opposite end is the bust of Helen: LA BELE ELLENE. Border of roses and leaves.

On the six sides are the following subjects:

(1) Fortune standing in a boat and holding up a mast with bellying sail: TOVT PAR FORTVNE LE ⚓ VA.

(2) An elderly man in fur cap and fur-lined cloak walks to left in a landscape: a purse hangs from his girdle, and he carries a stick:

ET MOI TEL QVE IE SVYS

IE LE FAIZ QVANT IE PVYS

A 50 ANS.

(3) A woman in a white linen head-dress holds out a rosary attached to her girdle:

QVANT ON LE ME PRE|SENTE

IE LE PRENS EN PACIANCE

A 40 ANS.

(4) An old man wearing a hood, cloak and high boots walks to left supported on a stick:

HELAS IESVS VR(AI)Y | DIEV DE GRACE

LE IE IEV D|AYMER FAICT ON ENCORES

A 80 ANS.

(5) An old woman in a mob-cap holding a stick in her right hand:

QVĀT DV IEV DAYMER ME | SOVVIĒT

LA LARME AVX I|EVLVLX ME VIĒN

A 70 ANS.

(6) A fool in cap and bells carrying a bauble over his left shoulder, and pointing to the left:

IL SEMBLE AV VILANT | PAR ABVZ

QVE LES IEVLX DAYMER SOVENT PERDVZ.

Plate XXII. French. 16th century.

H. 3 in. D. 4⅜ in. Magniac Collection (no. 390). The enamel upon the corners of this saltcellar is chipped. It may be by Couly Nouailher, see Introduction, p. 66. One of the two hexagonal saltcellars in the Wallace Collection at Hertford House has the same subjects.

67. SET OF SIX PANELS in grisaille: THE LORD'S PRAYER. On the panel to the left at the top, Our Lord is seen addressing the disciples in a landscape with a hill. Below is the legend.:

IHESVS · DICT · A · SES DISEIPSES · QVANT | VOUS PRIEREZ HE PARSEZ · PAS BEAV|COP MAIS PRIEZ AMSY 🌿 · MAT · (Matt. vi. 9.)

On the panel to the right the Virgin is seated with an open book on her knees between groups of seated and kneeling men. Behind her is a wall above which the dove is seen between clouds in the sky. Legend:

         TON ROVAINNE VIENNE A NOVS.

The left-hand panel in the middle shows a doctor in gown and flat cap preaching in a pulpit with a canopy, on which is the word VERITAS. Before the pulpit are seated women, behind whom men are standing. In the background is seen a courtyard in which a man and woman are drinking at a table. Legend:

     DONNE NOVS AVIOVRDHVY NOS|TRE PAIN COTIDIAN.

The corresponding panel on the right shows two men seated in the stocks in a prison, while a third in a plumed helmet proceeds to liberate the prisoner on the left. On the other side Our Lord in tunic and pallium advances with outstretched hands. Legend:

ET NOS PAIDŌNE · NOZ · OFFĒSES · AINSY | QVE · NOVS · PARDŌÑOS · A · CEVLX · Q̄ | NOVS · ONT · OFFENSE.

At the bottom on the left a devil seizes and scourges a seated figure, while flames envelop a building in the background. From the right, a woman advances, and above her the Almighty is seen holding a book and raising his right hand. Legend:

     ET · NE · NOVS · INDVIS · POINT · EN · TENTATION.

The bottom panel on the right has a death scene. A man lies on a bed by which are Our Lord, a man on crutches, a woman holding a taper, &c. In the foreground is a stool on which vessels stand: in the background are trees. Legend:

     MAIS · DELIVRE · NOVS · DV · MALIN · AMEN.

Plate. French, Limoges, 16th century.
All panels 4¾ in. × 3¾ in.

A set of similar panels was in the collection of the late W. Bemrose, Esq., Derby, and two panels from a third set (*Give us this day our daily bread*, and *Lead us not into temptation*) are in the Louvre. Colour is occasionally used to heighten the effect, chiefly red and yellow, and the panels have a good deal of gilding. Each is pierced with four holes. These panels were perhaps produced in the atelier of Couly Nouailher. In the Museum of the Hôtel Pincé at Angers there is a casket with figures in similar contemporary costumes, accompanied by inscriptions. It is signed C. N. and bears the date 1545 (see L. Gonse, *Chefs d'œuvres des Musées de France, sculptures, dessins, objets d'art* (Paris, 1904), fig. on p. 53).

68. PANEL: a scene from mythology or romance (?). Two men, one in a Phrygian cap, the other in a plumed helmet, are leading a white horse from the left; at the horse's head stands a bearded man in a cuirass. Beyond, on the right, are a boy, an old woman and a man, all gesticulating. The scene passes in a landscape with a building. A dog runs to right in the foreground.

French, Limoges, 16th century.

L. 15 in. From the Magniac Collection (no. 247).

The colouring of this panel is light, with a good deal of white, the chief tints being blue, green, yellow, and pink. The execution is coarse and the drawing careless, but spirited. At one period Léonard Limousin produced enamels with rather a pale scheme of colour on a white ground, and the present enamel appears to be by someone influenced by his style. Panels in a similar manner are in the Louvre and in the Musée de Cluny at Paris.

69. PAX in carved wooden frame: THE NATIVITY. On the right the Virgin kneels before a wattled crib in which the Child lies naked: behind are seen the heads of the ox and the ass. From the left, through an arched doorway, enters an old shepherd in short tunic and high boots: he holds a lighted candle in his left hand and with his right raises his low hat or cap. The scene is placed beneath a roofed colonnade; through this are seen a landscape with trees and the starry blue sky, in which the guiding star is seen sending out brilliant rays. The Virgin wears a purple tunic and blue mantle with an elliptical gold nimbus. The shepherd has a purple tunic and blue cap: the manger is turquoise blue. No foils are used.

Plate XXI. French, Limoges, 16th century.

H. $4\frac{1}{5}$ in. in frame, $8\frac{5}{8}$ in. B. $3\frac{1}{8}$ in.

The colouring and treatment of the trees recall enamels by Jean Courtois in the Waddesdon Bequest in the British Museum.

D.   8

70. PAX in gilt metal frame: THE ANNUNCIATION. On the right is the Virgin seated on a bench at a table, on which lie a book and scattered flowers: on the ground is a vase coloured pale blue and containing lilies. On the left the angel is seen flying down from the clouds with a lily in his left hand and holding his right up toward heaven. Behind the Virgin is a desk with a book and a bed with a canopy. The background is filled with architecture.

The Virgin's tunics are turquoise blue and blue respectively: her mantle is purple, and she has a radiating nimbus of gold. The garments of the angel are purple, blue and green, his wings green, blue and yellow. The tablecloth is turquoise blue, as is the coverlet of the bed; the canopy is light blue. The vase is blue, the clouds blue, the architecture purple, the ground a redder purple divided into squares by gold lines. Foils are freely used throughout, especially to heighten the colours of the garments.

The upper clouds, the top of the building and of the canopy, as well as both lower corners, have been restored.

Plate XXIII. French, Limoges, 16th century.
H. in frame 4⅞ in. B. 3¾ in. From the Magniac Collection (no. 519 A)?
In the style of Jean Limousin.

71. SHALLOW CUP with six lobes and two handles, on a hexagonal foot.

The bottom in the interior is painted with Cupid riding a lion to the right: above is the inscription onnia uinct amor; below, in the corner, the signature I. L.

The sides are brightly painted in the interior with flowers and birds in orange, blue, green, red and yellow, upon a white ground.

On the bottom is a landscape: a house with a bright red roof amid trees by a river. In the blue sky are red-brown clouds and a flight of distant birds.

On the exterior of the lobed sides are flowers and birds in purple, yellow, green and blue, with gold scroll designs, all on a black ground.

Limoges, 17th century.
D. 15¼ in.
Probably by Jacques Laudin I (A.D. 1627—1695), who sometimes signed with his initials only. He frequently painted in grisaille, his work recalling the

procedure of the sixteenth century. But Jacques Laudin II (A.D. 1663—1729) also signed I. L. and painted both in grisaille and colours.

An almost identical cup, with the same signature, Cupid and motto, is in the Ashmolean Museum at Oxford. They may both be compared with one of similar form in the Spitzer Collection, also signed I. L. (*La Collection Spitzer*, Vol. II, *Émaux, Prints*, no. 169). This is painted in grisaille and has in the centre Orpheus playing a violin, and round the sides animals, scrolls, and medallions: on the bottom is a landscape in colours. A large number of cups in the same style are preserved in various museums, about half a dozen being in the Louvre (Galerie d'Apollon). Other examples are at Milan and at Ravenna. An example in the Wallace Collection at Hertford House, also signed I. L., has in the centre a portrait of Louis XIII.

72. PANEL. Within an oval medallion, St Louis, in armour, and wearing a blue mantle with ermine, kneels before an altar on which are the nails and the crown of thorns. Behind him lie his own crown and sceptre. Below is the inscription SAINT LOVIS. The spandrels are ornamented with a foliate design in relief.

French, Limoges, 17th century.
H. 5½ in.
The chief colours are blue, green, orange, red and yellow.

73. ANOTHER, in similar style: St Eleanor in an ermine-lined mantle holding a palm in her left hand. Near her is a table, striped red and orange, on which are a crown and a sceptre. Below, SAINTE ELEONOR. Raised ornament in the spandrels, as in the previous number.

On the back is BᵀᴱNOVAILHER | EMAILLEVR | A LIMOGES.

French, Limoges, 17th century.
H. 4½ in.

74. ANOTHER, similar. St Elizabeth seated in a blue mantle with ermine cape, holding a fleur-de-lys sceptre. A beggar, only part of whose body is seen, approaches from the left: above him is a column draped by a green curtain. The spandrels have raised ornament.

On the back: *P. Nouailher | esmailleur | à Limoges.*

French, Limoges, 17th century.
H. 4¼ in. From the Magniac Collection (no. 247).

75. Ciborium of enamelled copper.

The foot is circular, and the broad stem is divided into two parts by a knop. The bowl is hemispherical and the lid is surmounted by a brass cross.

The stem, bowl and cover are ornamented with raised white lobes and gadroons upon a blue ground, the whole enriched with minute foliate designs in gold.

Plate XXIV. Venetian, 16th century.

H. 13⅜ in. From the Bateman Collection (Sale Catalogue, no. 187).

A paper label states that it was bought in Florence by Mr C. Redfern in 1857.

Painting under Glass (*Verre églomisé*).

(*See* Introduction, pp. 71 ff.)

76. Panel in a gilt wooden frame with a gable or pediment at the top, in which smaller panels are also set. In the middle the Virgin and Child are seated on a throne, the back surmounted by a gable and two pinnacles, and draped with a brocaded cloth. To right and left are two bearded apostles holding books, and two other saints. Below is the Annunciation, in two compartments bordered with quatrefoils filled out with black upon a crimson ground: the angel is in the left division, the Virgin upon the right. The whole panel is enclosed in a border ornamented with a running scroll in gold on a ground divided into sections alternately red and crimson.

Of the smaller panels, that in the pediment has Our Lord in the tomb; that above it, the Almighty making the gesture of benediction. The two panels to right and left have one a kneeling angel, the other the Virgin seated: beneath them are narrower panels with inscriptions in gold in Lombardic characters:

ECCE ANCILLA D(omini) and AVE GR(acia)E (plena).

Plate XXV. North Italian, 14th century.

Total height 33 in. H. of larger glass panel 10 in.

The frame is in the Sienese style, and of a later period than the glass. The upper part of the principal panel, including part of the body of the Virgin and the top of the throne, is very much rubbed. Silver foil was placed behind the gold foil in which the faces are executed in order to intensify the tone; this has oxidised, and thus unfortunately obscured the features.

The beautiful drawing of the faces indicates that this panel is the work of an artist of considerable merit.

77. PANEL: St Jerome kneeling in a cave to right before an altar on which are a crucifix, skull and scourge: his left hand rests upon the skull, and behind him lies the lion. In the background, seen through the opening of the cave, is a landscape in which is a church with a spire. The saint is nude but for a mantle covering his left shoulder and draped round the middle of his body.

Plate. German, 17th century.
H. 5 in.
The panel, which is executed in colours as well as gold, is in a black wooden frame with a border of glass, itself ornamented with églomisé scrolls in green, with red open flowers.

78. ANOTHER: the Virgin seated with the Child. Behind her on the left is St Elizabeth; in the foreground the young John the Baptist kisses the Child's hand. The Virgin wears a ruddy brown tunic and green mantle; St Elizabeth has a white hood.

Italian, early 18th century.
L. 6·75 in.
The back is protected by white foil, but the colouring is obscured down both sides. The subject is derived from a seventeenth-century picture by some master of the Eclectic school.

VARIOUS OBJECTS.

79. CENSER of gilt bronze. The cup is hexagonal with projections at the angles for the attachment of the chains: round the base it has a foliate design in low relief. The foot is hexagonal with ogee curves. The lid is pyramidal in three stages, one within the other, and there are turrets at all the corners. The lower stages are pierced with windows of three interlacing round-headed arches with tympanum and trefoil gable; the uppermost stage is pierced with trefoils.

Plate XXVI. 16th century.
H. 11½ in.

80. PRESSED TORTOISESHELL PANEL. Three-quarter figure of St Peter seated with clasped hands. On a rocky background above his head is a cock crowing, on his left are a book and keys.

German, 17th century.
H. 5⅛ in.
The minor art of producing designs by pressing tortoiseshell, horn or wood reduced to a soft condition into a mould chiefly flourished in the seventeenth and eighteenth centuries. The principal known artists are John Osborn, an Englishman working at Amsterdam in A.D. 1626, and John O'Brisset or Obrisset, the period of whose activity falls nearly a century later. Fine examples of their work may be seen in the British Museum (see C. H. Read, in *Some Minor Arts* by Sir A. H. Church, W. Y. Fletcher and others, London, Seeley, 1894, pp. 1—7).

81. OVAL LOCKET-RELIQUARY of gilt copper, with cardboard spaces for relics under glass on each side. On the exterior are two nielloed silver plates, that on one side having the bust of Pope Pius II, with legend PIVS II PONT. MAX, that on the other his arms (Piccolomini), with tiara and keys.

The frame, *Italian, 16th century.*
L. of frame 3⅜ in. From the Magniac Collection. The niello is modern.

82. WAX AGNUS DEI, circular.
Obverse. The lamb recumbent, supporting the flag with the right foot.
Below, the arms of Pius V.
Round the border: ECCE · A · DEI QVI TOLLIT · P · M · (*Ecce Agnus Dei qui tollit peccata Mundi*).
Reverse. The *Noli me tangere*.
Below, the inscription

PIVS · V · PONTIFEX
· MAXIMVS ·
· ANNO · I ·

In the border: NOLI · ME · TANGERE.
The wax disc is protected by two discs of carton with subjects in relief painted and gilded. One has the same design and inscription as the obverse on the wax, but instead of the arms of Pius V, those of Gregory XIII (Buoncompagni). The other has Our Lord in the tomb supported by two angels, with the cross

behind him. Below are again the arms of Buoncompagni, and in the border GREG · XIII · PONT · MAX.

The whole is in a circular wooden frame painted black with gilded oves and floral scrolls.

D. of wax disc 5 in. D. of frame 6·5 in.

The Agnus Dei was made from the wax of the Paschal Candle and blessed by the Pope the first Easter of his pontificate, and on every seventh anniversary. The present ceremonial dates from the sixteenth century, but the usage is said to go back as far as the ninth. The gilding and colouring of the Agnus Dei was forbidden after the year 1572. Among early surviving specimens are examples of the fourteenth century made in the pontificates of John XXII and Gregory XI (the latter in the Museum at Poitiers). An example which must be yet earlier was discovered with the relics of the Chapel of the *Sancta Sanctorum* at the Lateran not many years ago (P. Lauer, *Monuments Piot*, Vol. XV, 1906, p. 100 and pl. xi, 3). An example of Pius IV is in the Cluny Museum at Paris; and the British Museum has one of Clement XI (A.D. 1700—1721): numerous late examples are in the Vatican. The form and size have both varied: the earliest specimens appear to be the smallest, while the circular shape was at first preferred to the oval.

The wax Agnus Dei was considered to have a prophylactic or amuletic virtue in the Middle Ages, and fragments of it were worn in metal cases upon the person, especially by women. Matthew Paris, describing the fires at the Church of St Albans about A.D. 1235, deplores the want of efficacy of the Agnus blessed by the Pope placed on the summit of the tower (*Gesta Abbatis Johannis*, p. 142).

V. Gay, *Glossaire archéologique du Moyen Âge et de la Renaissance*, s.v. *Agnus Dei*. W. Henry in Cabrol's *Dictionnaire d'Archéologie Chrétienne et de Liturgie*, under the same title.

Apparently impressions with a similar design were made outside Italy by authorisation of the Pope. A matrix in the British Museum, of the fourteenth century, may be of this class (cf. also example found at Bristol, *Arch. Journal*, xxix, 1872, p. 361). The impressions being so highly valued, spurious matrices were soon made, and heavy penalties were awarded to those detected in their manufacture. By a statute of Henry VIII the possessor of a false matrix was subject to the penalties of *praemunire*; the second offence was treated as high treason.

83. WINE-GLASS on a high stem, the cup engraved with sprays, the stem containing twisted threads of white producing a spiral design.

English (?), 18th century.
H. 7 in.

84. BRONZE SPEAR-HEAD, leaf-shaped, with socket and holes for pin.

9th or 10th century B.C.

L. 8·7 in.

Cf. W. Greenwell in *Archaeologia* LXI, p. 460.

85. BRONZE; small figure of a ploughing-ox.

Italian, 8th—9th century B.C.

L. 2·62 in.

Perhaps part of a group representing a man ploughing.   Cf. Example in the British Museum.

Guide to the Exhibition illustrating Greek and Roman life, p. 206.

86—91. BRONZE; six statuettes of animals: goat, sheep, reindeer, panther, two dogs and a fish.

Graeco-Roman (?).

Average length 2—3 in.

Some of these figures are in a more conventional style and perhaps earlier than others.   While none appear to be so early as no. 85, some (e.g. the dogs) by their realistic style suggest a time almost as late as the Roman period. Such animals belong to the category of toys or ornaments.

92. BRONZE MIRROR engraved with four figures, Athene, Aphrodite and attendants.

Etruscan, 3rd century B.C.

L. 10·3 in.

93—96. BRONZE; FOUR SPIKED CYLINDERS from bits.

Greek, about 4th century B.C.

Largest diameter, 2 in.

These appear to be the "hedgehogs" (ἐχῖνοι) mentioned by Xenophon *De re eq.* X. 6 and illustrated upon complete bits in the British Museum (*Guide to the Collection illustrating Greek and Roman life,* fig. 211).

97. BRONZE EWER with high handle: unornamented.

Graeco-Roman, about 4th century.

H. 6·6 in.

98. BRONZE END OF A CHARIOT-POLE terminating in the head and fore quarters of a ram: rectangular socket.

Roman.

L. 7·4 in.

99.   BRONZE BELL, with loop at top; of oval section; without clapper.

Roman.
H. 3·6 in.

100.   BRONZE BELLS of rectangular section; loop at top; no clapper.

Roman.
H. 2·4 in. and 2·2 in.

101.   TRIPOD LAMP-STAND, bronze, terminating above in three short branches.

Graeco-Roman, 1st or 2nd century B.C.
H. 11·8 in.

102.   BRONZE STEELYARD (*statera*).

Roman.
L. 7·3 in.

103.   BRONZE EMBLEMA, in the form of a female bust: hollow at the back.

Roman.
H. 1·46 in.

104.   BRONZE LAMP-FILLER; hemispherical bowl with long straight channel or spout.

Late Roman.
L. 4·85 in.
The form may be compared with that of an example from Egypt in the Christian Room at the British Museum (*Cat. of Early Christian Antiquities*, no. 527).

105.   BRONZE; finial ornament with mask.

16*th century* (?).
D. 2·4 in.

106.   BRONZE MACE-HEAD; globular with three rows of knobs.

Uncertain date.
L. 2·6 in.

107. BRONZE; laureate head.

Modern.
H. 4·5 in.

ROMAN GLASS.

108. BOTTLE. Light-green glass. Neck narrow, slightly constricted where it joins the body. The rim of the neck made by the addition of a ring of glass. The base has a considerable conical kick ending in a hollow spike.
Condition, perfect: surface slightly iridescent.
Roman period. 1st century A.D. (?). Height 16·0 cm.
Original provenance unknown. Forman Collection.

109. BOTTLE. Light greenish-blue glass, with slight opalescence probably due to oxidization. Wide neck, the rim made by the addition of a ring of glass. Base nearly flat.
Condition, perfect: surface slightly iridescent.
Roman period. 1st century A.D. (?). Height 16·0 cm.
Original provenance unknown. Forman Collection.

CHINESE AND JAPANESE OBJECTS.

110. LOW VASE with cover and two handles, of cloudy green jade carved in relief. Round the outside of the bowl and cover are the Buddhist symbols. On the top of the lid is a dragon head, while lion heads adorn the handles.

Plate XXVII. Chinese. 18th century.
W. 7¼ in.

111. ANOTHER, of similar jade, with three feet and two handles with loose rings. On the body and cover are carved conventional scrolls of archaic type. On the top of the cover, which is in openwork, is an archaic dragon. The jade is very thin throughout.

Plate XXVII. Chinese. 18th century.
L. 8½ in.

112. CIRCULAR DISH OF CLOISONNÉ ENAMEL on copper, the chief ground-colour a turquoise blue. A central medallion has the Chinese character for Happiness (fuh), in red on white; round this are two dragons beyond which are borders of floral and geometrical design. The back has bamboo and prunus flowers within floral borders.

Japanese, 18th century (?).
D. 6·7 in.
The dish is probably Japanese, though a Chinese origin is not excluded. If Chinese the date would be somewhat earlier than that suggested.

113. IVORY NETSUKÉ; Benkei drawn in a rickshaw by an *Oni* accompanied by a *Tengu*. He is represented as a *Yamabushi* (wandering priest) and carries a conch shell on his back. On the base, a signature engraved upon a teapot.

Japanese, 19th century.
D. 1·6 in.
The legend will be found in H. Joly, *Legend in Japanese Art*, p. 20 (London, 1908).

114. IVORY NETSUKÉ, flat rectangular, carved in low relief upon one surface with a half-figure of Benkei holding a huge fish. Signed : *Ko gioku San.*

Japanese, 19th century.
L. 1·75 in.
Cf. Joly, as above.

115. ANOTHER, group in the round; an *Oni* carrying on his back a large tobacco-pouch, which a small *Oni* helps to support from behind : the toggle at the end of the cord of the pouch is carved to represent the No mask of Hanya. Signed : *Min koku.*

Japanese, 19th century.
H. 1·4 in.

116. ANOTHER; two *Oni* cleaning a large Chinese vase engraved with dragons. On the bottom of the vase a diminutive signature.

Japanese, 19th century.
L. ·2 in.

117. ANOTHER; a fisherman taking a fish from a large cylindrical basket in which are seen other fish and a crab. On the bottom of the basket is a signature.

Japanese, 19th century.
L. 1·85 in.

118. ANOTHER; a rat with a candle-end: on the candle a signature: *Tada mitsu.*

Japanese, 19th century.
L. 1·95 in.

EGYPTIAN ANTIQUITIES.

119. BOOK OF THE DEAD made for The Captain (ḥry) of the boats of the temple of Amon Rḗ, In·peḥuef·neḫt ⟨𓀀 𓏤 𓈖⟩ son of the captain of the boats of the temple of Amon Rḗ Ḗša·iḫt ⟨𓍝 𓏤⟩ written on a strip of papyrus 175 cm. long and from 37 to 38 cm. wide.

It consists of a few vignettes, or pictures, and short extracts from chapters of The Book of the Dead.

The text and pictures are enclosed within a rectangular border, the inner half plain, the outer red. The deceased is represented at both ends of the papyrus clad in white robes; his skin is dark brown where uncovered but shows pink through the outer garment.

The text is in vertical lines reading from right to left, portions of the text such as the titles are written in red. The writing is bold, and the pictures well drawn and brightly coloured.

At the right hand end of the papyrus is a picture of In·peḥuef·neḫt with his hands raised in adoration before a conventional shrine within which are the vignettes and text. Above and in front of him is part of the Introduction to the Negative Confession, his name and title, and his father's name and title. Ranged along the top of the cornice of the shrine are a number of figures ⟨𓁐⟩ with their names above them, which belong properly to "the Book of what is in Hades" (see Lefébure, *Tombeau de Séti I,* pls. XVII—XX).

The first part of the shrine is occupied by the 42 Assessors and the Negative Confession, followed by a "Book of becoming a swallow" and two vignettes, one above the other, the upper showing the swallow perched on a multi-coloured mound, the lower a squatting human figure with a swallow in the place of a head. This is succeeded by a short "Chapter of entering the region of sand" and a vignette representing two cynocephalous apes, the upper one facing to the left, the lower to the right. This is followed by a group of vignettes, in the upper one is the boat of Re in a backwater or harbour adored by two figures in priests' garments, while on the banks of the stream or harbour are the goddesses Isis and Nephthys. Below is a sign of life ('nḫ) with hands holding out bread offerings, flanked by two jackals, called "The Runner of the North," and "The Runner of the South." A short "Hymn to Rê at his setting" follows, and a scene showing In · peḥuef · neḥt adoring the sun which is about to be received into the arms of the sky goddess, while below are three pits between four flames, and below these again a tank about which the four flames are as a rule placed.

The papyrus seems to belong to the 18th Dynasty, but there are many points which indicate a later date; it should perhaps therefore be assigned to the 19th Dynasty.   [4001. 04]

120. CYLINDRICAL ALABASTER VASE, part of the foundation deposit of a building at Thebes built by Amenhetep II. Three vertical lines of inscription under a ⊏⊐ sign read from right to left: (here transposed)

The inscription is rather roughly incised and has been filled in with blue, traces of which remain.

18th Dynasty. Height 10·5 cm.   [4008. 04]

121. BLUE-GREEN GLAZED FAIENCE USHABTY made for Pa-dy-ise (Pȝ-dy-ys-t). Pillar up the back. The front is inscribed with Chap. VI of the Book of the Dead in 9 horizontal lines.

Good work of the Saite period. Height 17·5 cm.   [5014. 04]

122. GREEN GLAZED FAIENCE USHABTY made for Ptaḥ-hetep. Pillar at the back. The front inscribed with Chap. IV of the Book of the Dead in 9 horizontal lines.

Saite period. Height 18·0 cm. [5017. 04]

123. DULL GREEN GLAZED FAIENCE USHABTY made for Psemetek (Śmptk). Pillar at the back. The front is inscribed with Chap. VI of the Book of the Dead in 11 horizontal lines.

Good work; but the glazing poor. Saite period. Height 19·5 cm. [5016. 04]

124. GREEN GLAZED USHABTY made for Ḥor(?). Pillar at the back. The front inscribed with part of Chap. VI of the Book of the Dead in one vertical line.

Moderately good work of the Saite period. Height 14·5 cm. [5018. 04]

125. BLUE GLAZED FAIENCE STANDING FIGURE OF THE GODDESS SEḤMET, wearing a sun's disc and uraeus. The column or strip up the back is pierced for suspension and is inscribed

The face is well modelled, but the body is rather poor work. The feet are missing.

Saite period. Height 8·0 cm. [5011. 04]

126. GREEN GLAZED FAIENCE STANDING FIGURE OF THE GODDESS SEHMET or Bast (Bȝśt-t). The pillar at the back is pierced for suspension.

Poor work of the Saite period. Height 9·0 cm. [5012. 04]

127. BLUE GLAZED FAIENCE FIGURE OF THE GODDESS BAST (Bȝśt-t) seated on a throne holding a papyrus-sceptre, the upper part only being shown. The details of the sceptre and the panels of the throne are done with black glaze. At the back of the goddess's head is a loop for suspension. Height 7·5 cm. [5010. 04]

128. STANDING FIGURE OF THE GOD THOTH. Blue glazed faience.

Good work of the Saite period. The beak and lower part of the legs are missing. Height 10·0 cm.   [5007. 04]

129. SQUATTING CYNOCEPHALOUS APE. Blue glazed faience.
Very good work of the Saite period. Height 4·8 cm.
[5008. 04]

130. ISIS AND THE INFANT HORUS. Blue glazed faience.
Top of headdress missing. Rough work. Height 9·0 cm.
[5006. 04]

131. ISIS WITH THE INFANT HORUS. Bronze.
Saite period. Height including the tang 20·0 cm.   [5013. 04]

132. ISIS WITH THE INFANT HORUS. Serpentine. Very rough unfinished work. Traces of gilding on the face of the goddess.
Roman (?). Height 18·0 cm.   [6029. 04]

133. ANUBIS in the form of a jackal lying on the top of a shrine-shaped box. Bronze.
Roman period. Made in Italy (?). Length 15·0 cm.
"From Count d'Herisson collection."
[6030. 04]

134. PECTORAL in the form of the façade of a shrine. Part of the design is done with pieces of coloured glass let in and fixed with plaster. On one side Isis and Nephthys in the sacred boat adore the god Ḥepery in the form of a scarabaeus; on the other is the scarabaeus Ḥepery between a dd-t and a s; amulet.
The specimen is much damaged. 10·0 × 9·0 cm.
Forman collection.   [6028. 04]

135. STEATITE PECTORAL in the form of the façade of a shrine. Decorated partly by engraving the stone and partly by inlaying pieces of coloured glass held in position by plaster. These inlays have now fallen out. On one side Isis and Nephthys in the holy boat adore a shrine between two scarabaei, or ovals; on the other two priests adore a hawk-headed scarabaeus supported by another with outspread wings.

Ptolemaic or later.   10·0 x 10·0 cm.

Forman collection.   [6027. 04]

136. GREEN JASPER "HEART SCARAB." Made for Iuty (Yw-ty). Chap. XXX. B. of the Book of the Dead engraved on the base. New Kingdom. Length 7·2 cm.

Original provenance unknown.   [4002. 04]

137. SCHIST SCARAB, thickly coated with blue glaze. Roughly executed figures on the base. Poor work of Early New Kingdom date. Length 1·7 cm.   [4007. 04]

138. SCHIST SCARAB, originally green glazed. The design on the base consists of scarabaei with out-spread wings.

18th or 19th Dynasty.   Length 2·0 cm.   [4006. 04]

139. BLUE GLAZED FAIENCE SCARAB. Two crocodiles on the base. Rough work of the New Kingdom. Length 2·5 cm.
                                                    [4005. 04]

140. GREEN GLAZED SCARAB. On the base Horus, above two signs *pehty* facing each other. Length 1·9 cm.   [4004. 04]

141. HOLLOW BLUE GLAZED SCARAB, blackened over. The base is a separate plaque of blue glazed frit, with a lug pierced for suspension. On the plaque is a much defaced inscription in black glaze giving the name of the deceased.

20th Dynasty or later.   Length 7·5 cm.   [4003. 04]

ASSYRIAN AND BABYLONIAN ANTIQUITIES.

142. CLAY TABLET. Cuneiform inscription recording a loan of corn, dated 12th year of Artaxerxes I. 6·5 x 5·0 cm. [7001. 04]

143. CLAY TABLET. Cuneiform inscription recording a loan of corn with the names of the witnesses, dated 10th year of Darius. 6·25 x 5·0 cm.   [7002. 04]

INDEX

Achaemenian jewellery, 12–13
Adam, skull of, 97
Aegina, treasure from, 35
Agaune, S. Maurice d', enamelled ewer at, 45
Agnus Dei, no. 82
Ahin Posh tope, ornament from, 10
Alcester, tau cross from, 30
Alfred jewel, the, 20
Altötting, Rössl of, 60
Angermair, C., 57
Anglo-Saxon ivories, 30; enamels, 41; niello, 70
Annunciation, The, nos. 39, 70; to Shepherds, no. 40
Anubis, no. 133
Archbishop represented, 91, no. 35
Ardagh chalice, the, 46
Ardeshir, king, 9
Austria, enamels in, 39, 50, 62

Barbaric jewellery, 5–16, nos. 1–12
Bartlow, enamelled vase from, 38, 40
Basse taille, enamel in, 55
Bast or Sehmet, figure of, nos. 126–7
Becket, murder of, no. 41
Belgium, Roman enamels from, 39, 40
Bells, bronze, nos. 99–100
Betrayal, the, 42
Blois, Henry of, enamel of, 49
Boabdil, swords of, 45
Bodleian Library, ivory carving in, 23, 89
Bone, Henry, 69
Bottles, Roman glass, nos. 108–9
Byzantine ivory carvings, 26–7, nos. 36–38; jewellery, 15

Candlesticks, 100, 108

Canosa, glass bowls from, 71
Carolingian art, *see* Frankish art
Caskets, ivory, 24, 53, no. 36; enamelled, no. 58
Castel Trosino, Teutonic ornaments from, 8
Catherine, Saint, no. 43
Caucasus, enamels from, 35
Cellini, 55
Cennini, Cennino, 73
Censer, no. 79
Chalice, no. 6
Chariot-pole, end of, no. 98
Childeric, sword of, 7
China, influence of, 11; jade vases from, nos. 110, 111
Chinese enamel, 11
Church, Sir A. H., 33, 34, 36
Ciborium, no. 59
Claire, Godefroid de, 50
Cloisonné, *see* Enamel
Conques, reliquaries at, 47, 49
Courajod, L., 20
Court, Jean de, 67; Suzanne de, 67
Courtois or Courteys, Pierre, 66; Jean, 67
Craft, W., 69
Crucifixion, the, nos. 38, 39, 41, 42, 55, 57, 59
Cuneiform tablets, nos. 142–3
Cynocephalous ape, no. 129

Dashur, jewellery from, 14
de Laulne, Étienne, 46
Descent from the Cross, no. 42
Didier, Martin, 66
Die, Master of the, 62
Dillon, E., 33, 71
Dinant, enameller's furnace near, 39
Diptychs, "Composite," 23

Echini, nos. 93–96

Églomiser, derivation of the word, 76

Egypt, inlaid jewellery of, 14; absence of enamel in, 33

Elizabeth, St, nos. 43, 74

Émaux de niellure, 52

Emmanuel, type, 90

Enamels, 32–71; Belgian, 48–50; Byzantine, 41–43; Caucasian, 35; Celtic, 35–37; Champlevé, 48–54; Cloisonné, 11, 41, no. 112; Encrusted, 58; English, 41, 53, 54; German, early, 48–51, nos. 56, 58; German, late, 68; Greek, 34, 58; Hungarian, 45; Irish, 40; Limoges, 48, 51–2, nos. 47–57; Low Countries, 62–68; Moorish, 44–5; Mycenaean (?), 35; Oriental, 69; Painted, 59–69, nos. 63–75; Roman, 38–40, nos. 44–46; Russian, 43–4, 54; Spanish, 53, 56; Translucent, 55; Venetian, 61

Enamelled dish, no. 112

Enamelling in openwork, 46; on glass, 46

English enamels, 41, 53, 54, 57

Engraved gems, 81–84

Entombment, the, no. 43

Ephesus, ivory carvings from, 16

Evangelists, symbols of the, 91

Evans, Sir A., 42

Ewer, bronze, no. 97

Farley Heath, enamels from, 38

Faversham, brooch from, 5, no. 4

Filarete, 61

Finiguerra, 71

Flagellation, the, 42, 59

Florence, enamelled crozier at, 49; translucent enamels at, 55

Fondi d'oro, 72, 73

Foucquet, Jehan, 60

Foundation deposit of Amenhetep II, no. 120

France, early enamels from, 39; Byzantine enamels in, 43; enamelling on glass in, 46; enamels in *basse taille* from, 56; enamels on relief from, 58

Frankfort, ivory panel at, 26, 92

Frankish art, 19 ff., nos. 9–11, 34, 35

Franks, Sir A. W., 40

Gems, engraved, 81–84, nos. 12–31

Germany, early enamels from, 39; Byzantine enamels in, 43; Cloisonné enamels of, 44; Enamels on relief from, 58; Inlaid jewellery from, 8, 9; Painted enamels from, 68; Translucent enamels of, 56, 57

Gilded glasses, 72, 73

Giovanni Pisano, ivory statuette by, 31

Glass, 71–76, no. 83; *see also* Gilded glasses

Gnostic gems, 82, 83

Godwin, seal of, 30

Gold Cup, the Royal, 56

Gold ornaments, prehistoric, nos. 1, 2

Goldschmidt, A., 22, 28, 88

Goths, transmitters of a style of jewellery, 9

Gourdon, treasure of, 7

Graeven, H., 27

Gran, enamel at, 58

Grandisson, Bishop, ivory carvings made for, 30

Gregory the Great, gifts of, 8

Gregory XIII, Pope, no. 82

Gryphons represented, no. 36

Guarrazar, votive crowns from, 7, 8

Harwood, enamels from, 38

Heraclius, 73

Hildesheim, sculpture at, 28

Horus and Isis, figure of, nos. 130–2

Hugo, Frère, of Oignies, 70

Hungary, enamels in, 45, 58

Illuminations, early Irish, 41

India, gold ornament from, 10

"Inlaid jewellery," 5–16

Innsbruck, cloisonné dish at, 44

Intarsia, 96

Ionia, ivory carvings from, 16

Ireland, enamels of, 40, 46; early illuminations of, 41

Isis and the infant Horus, nos. 130–2

Italy, early enamels from, 40; translucent enamels of, 55, 56; painted enamels of, 60, 61

Ivory carvings, 16–32, nos. 32–43; colouring of, 31, 32

Jade vases, nos. 110, 111

Japanese enamel, no. 112; ivory carvings, nos. 113–118

Jean de Limoges, 52
Jerome, Saint, no. 77
Jerusalem Chamber, retable in, 74
Jewellery, 5–16, nos. 1–12
Jutish brooches, 79

Kent, Teutonic jewellery from, 5
Kertch, Teutonic jewellery from, 9
King's Lynn, enamelled cup at, 59
"Kip," 64
Kloster Neuburg, enamels at, 50
Koban, enamels from, 35
Kondakoff, N., 43

La Guierche, vase from, 39
Lamp-filler, no. 104
Lamp-stand, no. 101
Last Judgment, no. 39; Supper, no. 65
Laudins, the, 67
Layard, Sir H., 13
Limoges, champlevé enamels of, 48, 51, 52; painted enamels of, 59–69
Limousin, Léonard, 65; Jean, 67, no. 70; François, 67
Linear style, 21, 22
Lord's Prayer, illustrated, no. 67
Louis, Saint, no. 72
Love, triumph of, 66

Mace-head, bronze, no. 106
Magi, Adoration of, nos. 63, 64
Majestas Domini, 90
Mandorla, the, 90
Manuscripts, illuminated, influence of, 24, 25
Marcantonio, 62
Merovingian art, see Frankish art
Merton, Walter de, 52
Meuse, champlevé enamels of the, 48–51
Miracles, represented, 85
Mirror, bronze, no. 92
"Monkey beaker," the, 62
Montpellier, enamels of, 56
Monvaerni, 63
Monza, book-cover at, 8
Munich, Byzantine enamels at, 43
Mycenaean enamel, 25

Nativity, the, nos. 40, 69
Netsukés, nos. 113–118
Niello, 69–71

Nimrûd, inlaid ivory from, 13, 14
Northumbria, art of, 20
Nouailher, B., no. 73; Couly, 66, no. 66, 67; P., no. 74
Nubia, enamels from, 41

Ognabene, Jacopo d', 55
Orfèvrerie cloisonnée, see Inlaid jewellery
Orvieto, enamelled reliquaries at, 55, 56.
Our Lord, represented, nos. 32, 33, 34, 37, 38, 39, 40, 41, 42, 43, 47, 54, 55, 57, 59, 61, 63, 64, 65, 67, 69, 78
Oxus, treasure of the, 12

Painting, under glass, 71–76
Pallium, the archiepiscopal, 94
Papyrus of In·pehuef·neht, no. 119
Passion, scenes from the, nos. 42, 59; instruments of the, nos. 39, 61
Pectoral, nos. 134–5
Penicaud, Nardon, 63; Jean, I, II, III, 64–5
Persia, jewellery from, 8, 9, 12, 13
Peter, Saint, no. 80
Petrossa, treasure of, 8
Petruci, Andrea, no. 61
Pinguente, enamelled vessel from, 39
Pistoia, silver altar of, 55
Pius II, Pope, no. 81
  ,, V, Pope, no. 82
Plantagenet, Geoffrey, enamel of, 50
Poitiers, Byzantine reliquary at, 41
Poncet, H., 67
Pouan, treasure of, 7
Prehistoric gold ornaments, nos. 1, 2

Rainbow, as throne of Christ, 90
Ravenna, gold armour at, 8
Reymond, Pierre, 65, 66
Rhayader, enamels from, 40
Rhine, champlevé enamels of, 48–51
Risano, enamel from, 42
Rudge Cup, the, 38
Russia, enamels of, 43, 44, 54; jewellery from, 9, 12

Salutation, the, no. 39
Sancta Sanctorum, Chapel of the, 20, 41
Sassanian gems, 83, 84
Scarab, nos. 136–41
Sculpture influenced by ivory carvings, 18

Sehmet, figure of, nos. 125–6
Siberia, jewellery from, 12
Sicily, cloisonné enamels of, 44
Siena, chalice from, 108
Silos, casket from, 53
Sparta, early ivories from, 16
Spear-head, bronze, no. 84
Standon, enamels from, 38
Statuettes, bronze, nos. 85–91
Steelyard, no. 102
Stoke d'Abernon, enamel at, 53
Susa, jewellery from, 12–13
Symmachi, Diptych of, 24, 89
Syria, artistic influence of, 19

Textile ornament, influence on sculpture,
  17, 18
Theophanu, 26
Theophilus, 73
Thoth, figure of, no. 128
Tournai, reliquary at, 50

Toutin family, the, 68

Ushabty, nos. 121–4
Utrecht Psalter, the, 25

Venetian enamels, 61
Venice, Byzantine enamels at, 43
Veroli, casket from, 27
Verre églomisé, 71–76
Viking torc, no. 2
Virgin, coronation of the, no. 40
Vöge, W., 28

Way, A., 53
Werdenberg'scher Pokal, the, 62
Westminster Abbey, retable from, 74
Willelmus, Frater, 49
Wittislingen, jewels from, 8
Wolfsheim, gold ornament from, 9
Wykeham, William of, crozier of, 57

CAMBRIDGE: PRINTED BY JOHN CLAY, M.A. AT THE UNIVERSITY PRESS

Plate 1

Prehistoric and Early Teutonic Jewellery

Plate 11

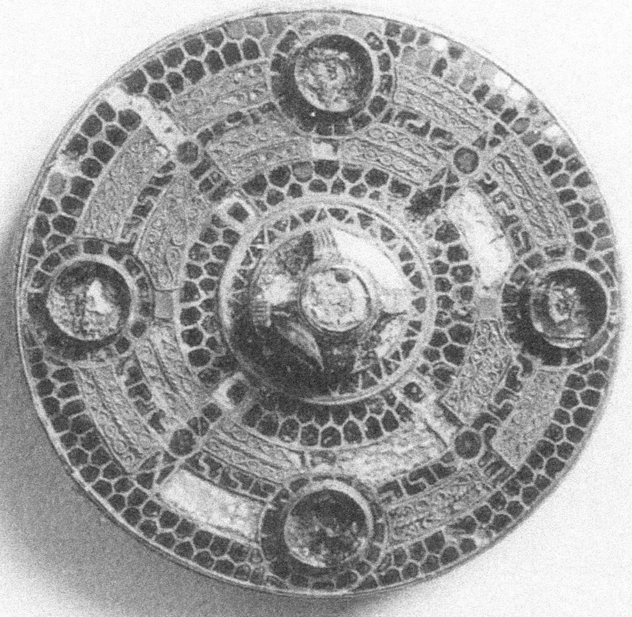

Gold brooch from Faversham; 7th century

Frankish buckle; 8th century

Plate III

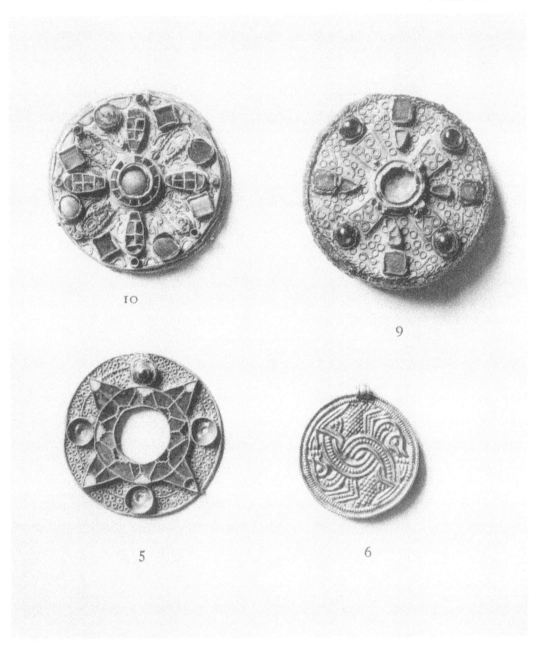

10

9

5

6

Jutish and Frankish jewellery of the 7th and 8th centuries

Plate IV

32, 33. Carved ivory panels; 6th century

Plate V

34. Carved ivory panel ; Carolingian, 9th century

Plate VI

35. Carved ivory panel; Carolingian, 9th century, with photograph of the
companion panel at Frankfort

Plate VII

36. Carved ivory casket with intarsia; 12th century

Plate VIII

37, 38.   Carved ivory panels ; Byzantine, 11th—12th century

Plate IX

39. Carved ivory diptych ; French, 14th century

Plate X

Ivory carvings; French, 14th century

Plate XI

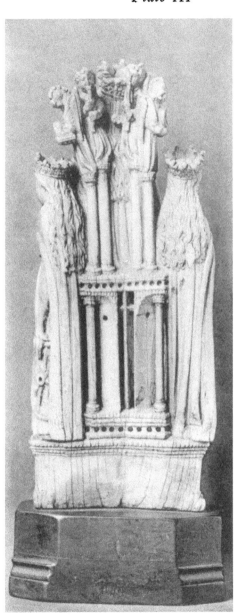

43. Carved ivory group; Spanish, 16th century

46

45

44

Roman enamel; 3rd century

Plate XIII

49, 50. Enamelled fragments ; Limoges, 12th century

Plate XIV

52. Enamelled end of a reliquary; Limoges, 13th century

Plate XV

55. Enamelled panel from a book-cover; Limoges, 13th century

Plate XVI

56. Enamelled plaques of a book-cover; Limoges, 13th century

Plate XVII

58. Casket with embossed silver and enamels; Rhenish, 12th century

Plate XVIII

59.   Enamelled ciborium; Limoges, 14th century

Plate XIX

60. Enamelled brass candlestick; English, 17th century

Plate XX

61.   Enamelled chalice ; Italian, late 14th century

Plate XXI

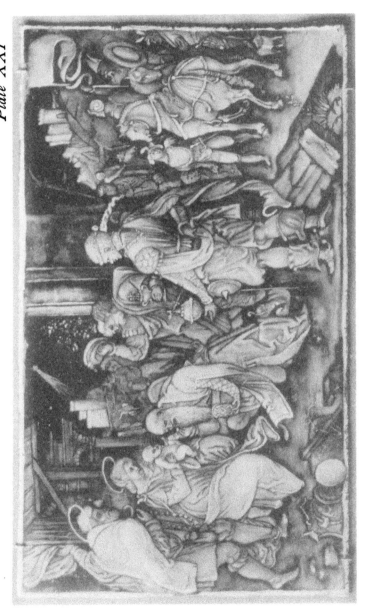

64. Painted enamel, The Adoration of the Magi; Limoges, 16th century

Plate XXII

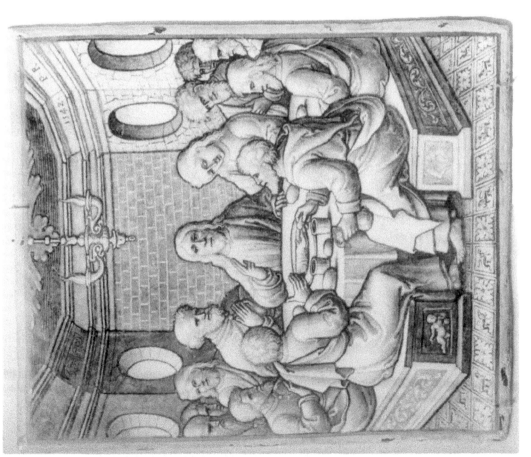

65, 66. Painted enamels; Limoges, 16th century

Painted enamels; Limoges, 15th and 16th centuries

Plate XXIV

75. Enamelled ciborium; Venetian, 16th century

Plate XXV

76. Painting under glass; Italian, 14th century

Plate XXVI

79.   Bronze censer; 16th century

Plate XXVII

110, 111. Jade vases; Chinese, 18th century

For EU product safety concerns, contact us at Calle de José Abascal, 56–1°,
28003 Madrid, Spain or eugpsr@cambridge.org.

www.ingramcontent.com/pod-product-compliance
Ingram Content Group UK Ltd.
Pitfield, Milton Keynes, MK11 3LW, UK
UKHW030901150625
459647UK00021B/2678